How to Open & Operate a Financially Successful

CONSULTING BUSINESS

With Companion CD-ROM

D1509134

Foreword by Janet Crenshaw Smith,
cofounder and president, Ivy Planning Group

HOW TO OPEN & OPERATE A FINANCIALLY SUCCESSFUL CONSULTING BUSINESS WITH COMPANION CD-ROM

Library of Congress Cataloging-in-Publication Data
Lorette, Kristie, 1975-
How to open & operate a financially successful consulting business : with companion CD-ROM / by Kristie Lorette.
p. cm.
Includes bibliographical references and index.

ISBN-13: 978-1-60138-016-6 (alk. paper)
ISBN-10: 1-60138-016-X (alk. paper)

1. Business consultants. 2. New business enterprises. 3. Small business--Management. I. Title. II. Title: How to open and operate a financially successful consulting business.
HD69.C6L57 2010
001--dc22
                    2008032590

Printed in the United States

PEER REVIEWER: Marilee Griffin • mgriffin@atlantic-pub.com
EDITORIAL INTERN: Shannon McCarthy • smccarthy@atlantic-pub.com
PROOFREADER: Amy Moczynski • amoczynski@atlantic-pub.com
FRONT COVER DESIGN: Meg Buchner • megadesn@mchsi.com
BACK COVER DESIGN: Jackie Miller • millerjackiej@gmail.com

Printed on Recycled Paper

We recently lost our beloved pet "Bear," who was not only our best and dearest friend but also the "Vice President of Sunshine" here at Atlantic Publishing. He did not receive a salary but worked tirelessly 24 hours a day to please his parents. Bear was a rescue dog that turned around and showered myself, my wife, Sherri, his grand-parents Jean, Bob, and Nancy, and every person and animal he met (maybe not rabbits) with friendship and love. He made a lot of people smile every day.

We wanted you to know that a portion of the profits of this book will be donated to The Humane Society of the United States. *–Douglas & Sherri Brown*

The human-animal bond is as old as human history. We cherish our animal companions for their unconditional affection and acceptance. We feel a thrill when we glimpse wild creatures in their natural habitat or in our own backyard.

Unfortunately, the human-animal bond has at times been weakened. Humans have exploited some animal species to the point of extinction.

The Humane Society of the United States makes a difference in the lives of animals here at home and worldwide. The HSUS is dedicated to creating a world where our relationship with animals is guided by compassion. We seek a truly humane society in which animals are respected for their intrinsic value, and where the human-animal bond is strong.

Want to help animals? We have plenty of suggestions. Adopt a pet from a local shelter, join The Humane Society and be a part of our work to help companion animals and wildlife. You will be funding our educational, legislative, investigative and outreach projects in the U.S. and across the globe.

Or perhaps you'd like to make a memorial donation in honor of a pet, friend or relative? You can through our Kindred Spirits program. And if you'd like to contribute in a more structured way, our Planned Giving Office has suggestions about estate planning, annuities, and even gifts of stock that avoid capital gains taxes.

Maybe you have land that you would like to preserve as a lasting habitat for wildlife. Our Wildlife Land Trust can help you. Perhaps the land you want to share is a backyard— that's enough. Our Urban Wildlife Sanctuary Program will show you how to create a habitat for your wild neighbors.

So you see, it's easy to help animals. And The HSUS is here to help.

2100 L Street NW • Washington, DC 20037 • 202-452-1100
www.hsus.org

Dedication

To my Boo Boo, who always makes me strive for the bigger and better things life has to offer and who is always there to share it with me.
I love you.

Table of Contents

Chapter 3: Planning a Successful Leap into Consulting — 61

Chapter 4: Putting Your Business Plan in Writing — 85

Chapter 5: Setting Your Fees — 105

Chapter 6: The Legalities of Starting Your Business — 133

Foreword

S o, you think you want to start a consulting firm? Begin by
reading this book. *How to Open & Operate a Financially Successful Consulting Business* provides the practical advice you need
to launch, manage, and grow a consulting firm. And beyond that,
Kristie Lorette challenges you to answer some important questions. Take time to ask yourself the tough questions that she pos-
es in chapters 1 and 2. For example, are you passionate about
problem solving? The best consultants find genuine delight in
solving their clients' problems. They are naturally curious. Even
during their "down time," they find they must resist the urge to
solve even their friends' problems. Is that you? Consider also, are
you someone people trust and respect? Many people may listen
to your advice and counsel when it is free, but do you have the
skills and reputation that will drive people to pay for your advice? A good consultant asks his or her client, "Have I earned the
right to return next week?"

How to Open & Operate a Financially Successful Consulting Business provides a logical framework to build your business plan. It offers considerations, guidelines for operating a success services business, insightful case studies, and even marketing tips and tactics.

When I started Ivy Planning Group with my husband and cousin more than 19 years ago, we had big dreams. But the journey from startup to multi-million dollar firm did not come without its challenges. We had excellent credentials, corporate-tested skills, and the "entrepreneurial bug." But we did not have a resource like this. Kristie Lorette has assembled the considerations, guidelines, and tips all in one place — the rest is up to you.

— *Janet Crenshaw Smith*

Janet Crenshaw Smith is cofounder and president of Ivy Planning Group (Ivy), a 19-year-old management consulting and training company that specializes in diversity, strategy, and change management. Ivy is recognized as one of the Top 50 Diversity-owned companies by DiversityBusiness.com; it was a *Black Enterprise Magazine* Emerging Company of the Year Finalist; and it received the *Working Woman* magazine Entrepreneurial Excellence Award. Minority Business & Professionals Network, Inc. named Smith one of "Fifty Influential Minorities in Business." *Profiles in Diversity Journal* featured

Smith in its *Women of Initiative* issue naming her one of "47 Women Worth Watching."

A native of Chicago's south side, Smith received her bachelor's degree from Harvard University and started her professional career at IBM Corporation where she held a number of marketing and management positions including manager of executive consulting services. She lives in Maryland with her husband/business partner, Gary A. Smith Sr., and their three sons.

Introduction

Deciding to become a consultant can be a big and exciting decision in your life and in your career. No matter what has propelled you toward taking this step, being a business consultant can be a powerful and rewarding experience because it puts you in the driver's seat of your own destiny, and is the means by which you can alter your career and financial future. Imagine how empowered you will feel as you set your own schedule, make your own decisions, and help clients answer questions and overcome challenges that they cannot handle on their own. As a consultant, you are the expert in your field, and you can pull the answers from your own bank of knowledge and experience to solve the problem or help the client work through their situation in an effective and productive manner.

You may possess the knowledge you need to launch a consulting business in your area of expertise, but starting a consulting business also requires you to learn how to become a business owner.

Once you determine this is the right step for you, then you also need detailed instructions on how to make it happen to ensure success.

To become a successful consultant, you must possess several key qualities: first, you must be an expert in a field. Second, you need to know when to listen to your clients. Third, you also need to be perceptive enough to pick up on the little things, and you need to be professional about the way that you convey your message. Lastly (and most importantly) you must be able to run your own business successfully.

How to Use this Book

How to Open & Operate a Financially Successful Consulting Business includes everything you need to know to start your business venture off on the right path — and to continue driving the business on the road to success. The first part of the book provides you with the tools, resources, and self-assessments you need to evaluate your personal and financial situation. If the time is not right, then you will learn what to do to make it viable for you to start a consulting business. After you know everything about timing the start of your business, the rest of the book covers the various steps you need to take to establish and run a financially successful consulting business.

Each chapter of the book covers what you need to know to build the foundation of each aspect of your business. From the different legal entity options for setting up the business (sole proprietorship or corporation) to marketing your business and how to handle clients, you will learn all of the things you need to know and be aware of to create as successful a consulting business as possible.

The beginning of each chapter includes a bullet point list that previews the topics covered in the upcoming chapter. This sets your expectations for what information you will walk away with once you have completed the chapter. Scattered throughout the chapter you will find checklists, tips, and warnings directly related to the topic at hand. There is no reason for you to reinvent the wheel and make the same mistakes those consultants who came before you have made. Heeding these warnings and using the advice provided streamlines the process for you so you can avoid making the same common mistakes that many new consultants make.

Keep an open mind as you read through the next 12 chapters. While owning your own business means you are your own boss, you still have to be accountable for your actions in order to be successful. Knowledge is power, and if you take what you learn from this book and apply it to your business then you are sure to create a powerful business. You are reading this book because you have an interest in becoming a consultant, so soak up all of the information you can so that it winds up being a positive venture. Financial and personal situations, objectives, and goals vary from person to person, so you will need to mold and adjust the advice to fit your particular situation. Use the information in this book to learn the benefits and disadvantages for each aspect of the consulting world. Then, use this information to make a personal decision for what is the right option for you.

Chapter 1

Timing is Everything;
So is Experience

In this chapter, you will:

- Learn the top reasons individuals become consultants and determine your own reasons for seeking a consulting career.

- Figure out how to determine if the timing is right to launch your consulting business.

- Uncover and analyze the personal, professional, and financial considerations of starting and running a consulting business.

- Take a self-assessment test on whether consulting is the career for you.

A consultant is someone who provides expert advice and guidance in exchange for a fee, and the reasons people become consultants vary. The great thing about consultants is that consulting options are as varied as the choices on a menu. Consultants come from different backgrounds, live in different areas, have different work experiences, and can range from the landscaping industry to feasibility consultants that help nonprofit organizations determine if they can raise the amount of money they need to tackle a project. In essence, consulting opportunities are almost limitless.

One of the first questions you need to answer before starting your businesses is: Why do you want to become a consultant? For many, the answer to this question is freedom. Most individuals who venture out on their own to open a business do it because they want to be their own boss, make their own hours, and do what they want without having to answer to a boss. Being a consultant provides you with that freedom.

Reasons to Become a Consultant

Take a look at some of the common reasons people choose to become consultants and see if your reasons are the same. While this section covers some of the common reasons consultants are born, if you do not see the reason you want to be a consultant here, it does not mean that you are not ready to become a consultant. Be sure to consider your own reasons and how becoming a consultant would benefit you.

1. Put your talent to good use

Everyone has an area of expertise they are passionate about, whether it is dogs, marketing, or streamlining manufacturing processes. One of the top reasons people become consultants is that they have a talent that is being stifled in their current career, and they are ready to unleash that talent and finally put it to good use. For some, their area of expertise is a hobby or more of a personal interest than that of a professional nature, but by no means does this mean that you should rule it out as a consulting option.

If you have worked as a restaurant manager for the last 20 years, then it is probably safe to say that nobody knows the ins and outs of the restaurant business better than you do. Rather than continue to manage the restaurant, why not spread your wealth of knowledge to a greater number of restaurants — helping them streamline the serving process, create superior customer experiences, and boost their bottom lines — rather than continue to serve only the current restaurant for which you work? Or maybe you have worked in marketing in various roles and for various companies. Over the past 15 years, you have seen what works when it comes to creating, implementing, and tracking marketing campaigns. You eat, sleep, and breathe marketing. You have the keen ability to look at a company's offerings and create a strategic marketing plan that can help them sell and increase revenues like there is no tomorrow. You can apply this talent, share it with numerous companies, and make money doing it.

Consider what areas of expertise you have and determine whether there is a market that needs fulfillment. Will someone pay you to design his or her garden and landscaping? Will someone pay you to teach him or her how to train a dog? Will someone pay you to become the marketing arm of a company? If the answer is yes to your question, then there may be a need you can fulfill in the market and make money in the process.

2. Layoffs

Especially since the downturn in the economy that started in 2007, layoffs are eminent for many employees of companies — especially those that have been around for multiple years. When companies downsize, it is often the highest-paid (and most-experienced) individuals who get cut first because it helps companies cut costs quickly and easily. In fact, many of the individuals who get laid off might have been contemplating forging out on their own for years, and getting laid off may be just the kick in the butt they need to go out on their own and turn their talents into a business.

In a tough economy, consultants can prosper while other companies falter. Think about it logically: A company that is downsizing still needs talented individuals to help it conduct business. It is much cheaper for a company to outsource their accounting, sales, marketing, and other needs than it is to have a full-time or part-time employee on staff to do it for them. A company does not have to pay a consultant's health insurance, fund a 401(k), or provide a desk, telephone, and computer for the consultant to use. A company pays a consultant on a per-project basis, which saves the company a substantial amount of money. This opens the door for you to apply your talent and fill a need a company has that can earn you a profit in the process.

If being laid off from your job is staring you in the face or you have already experienced a layoff, you may be able to find safety and security as a consultant. Some laid-off employees even end up working as consultants for the same company that let them go in the first place. In today's ever-changing economy, almost any type and size business can terminate its employees without advanced notice or a severance package. Becoming a consultant can be the solution to this problem for you. In fact, when you become a consultant, you get to choose your clients as much as they get to choose you. You may even be the one firing clients rather than the other way around. In many situations, you earn more money as a consultant than working as an employee for a company — even when the work is the same. Not only does consulting eliminate the layoff factor but it also can increase your income.

3. Become your own boss

Becoming a consultant is not only about venturing into a new career. It is also about becoming a business owner. So one of the top reasons why individuals turn to consultant work instead of working as an employee is they are tired of applying their talent and skills into making money for someone else. Consulting allows you to use your skills and talent to turn a profit for yourself and for your family.

Being your own boss allows you to make your own decisions. From working the schedule you want (even if it is in the middle of the night) to removing the cap from your potential income, being your own boss puts you in control of your career. Not having to answer to someone else on a daily basis removes many of the constraints that hold a typical employee back from reaching the peak of their success. Becoming a consultant positions you to earn your own profits and create your own destiny.

4. Create additional income

Even those who wish to continue working a full-time or part-time job can become a consultant in order to generate more income. You may even be able to consult in the same line of work as what you are doing as an employee. For example, you work as a loan officer at a local bank and are knowledgeable when it comes to the financial world. You may be able to use this knowledge and experience to offer advice as a financial columnist for a personal finance publication where you answer the questions that readers send in on personal finance topics. This consulting position allows you to set your own schedule, work around your other engagements, and continue working at your full-time position. In addition, you can work where and when you want to — even if it is at 3 a.m. sitting in your pajamas.

5. You want to move above the glass ceiling

Every company has a limit on how high you can reach as an employee. Even if your final position with a company is president and CEO, you cannot go any higher than this position. No matter how hard you work and how many hours you put in, there is a limit on how far you can go with a company. Because you are in control of everything from how many hours you put in to how much you charge a client, your income and your goals can reach way beyond the confines of a typical company infrastructure if you choose to open your own consulting business.

CASE STUDY: TRANSITIONING FROM EMPLOYEE TO SELF-EMPLOYED

```
Left Field Solutions, LLC
Geoffrey P. Lamdin
Brunswick, ME 04011
207-522-7900
www.consultexpertise.com
```

Left Field Solutions, LLC focuses on catalyzing, facilitating, and fostering innovation, primarily in the clean-tech and renewable energy industries. Its founder, Geoffrey Lamdin, provides strategic creativity, tactical, and operational guidance for companies from concept to marketing, so the services help assist startups and established firms.

What led Lamdin to start his own consulting business were the continuous layoffs he experienced from his previous jobs. Being self-employed was also a way for him to become house-dad to his two kids, allowing his wife to continue building her career as a professional educator.

The timing for transitioning from an employee to opening his own consulting business was not entirely optional, but Lamdin took advantage of his being "released" from his last employee role to become a house-dad. He enjoyed being responsible to himself, although in the past he preferred and sought out projects that benefited more from a team approach.

His employee experience was limited primarily in not-for-profits, so his early consulting days focused on the independent sector, which gave him a baseline. Lamdin believes that being his own boss has provided him a license to be a lifelong learner. Asking questions, observing, and being intuitive have become acquired skills.

Timing Your Transition

From what is going on in the economy to what is going on in your personal and professional life, there are factors to timing your move from your current employment situation into the world of consulting. While there is no conclusive test that provides a definitive answer that says the time is now, you need to assess all of the personal, financial, and experiential aspects of your personal situation as you work your way through the decision making process.

Professional considerations

There is no rule that says you cannot love what you do as a career. In fact, working as a consultant probably requires you to love what you do more because you are the owner of the business, as well as the worker bee. Because consulting will be your career, the first thing you need to consider is your professional situation. If you want to be a successful consultant, you have to have the skills, resources, and experience required to perform the job you are signing on to do.

You need to possess a unique selling proposition (USP), a benefit or a reason for companies to want and need to hire you as a consultant. For example, if your full-time career has been in the automotive industry, but you want to start your professional consulting career in landscaping, you have to have the expertise in landscaping to make it happen, and you have to sell that expertise to the company. It is important that you be realistic when you are assessing your move into the world of consulting. A solid foundation of experience is essential to launching and maintaining a successful consulting career. Take this self-assessment to see if you have what it takes to be able to fulfill the professional requirements for becoming a consultant.

Subject expert: Knowledge is imperative, so you have to be an expert on the subject, niche, or industry for which you are consulting. For example, if your target audience is mortgage brokers and loan officers, then you have to have knowledge of the mortgage and lending industry. If you want a company to hire you, you have to show the management responsible for hiring that you are an expert in the field and that you can help them resolve their problem or take their business to the next level.

Degrees, licensing, or certifications: In some professions, a license, degree, or related certifications can be an important factor. These pieces of paper can add value to your services as a consultant and may make the difference of being hired or being passed over for a consulting opportunity. Licenses, certifications, and degrees are proof of your expert-level of experience and knowledge. Some professions require these items by law, but other professions can use it to their advantage to charge more money or convince a client to hire them. *Chapter 6 covers more of the legalities of licenses and other legal steps you may need to take to become a consultant and to open your consulting company.* You can also update and refresh your skills with continuing education classes and courses.

Professional references: Next, consider whether you have the professional references to back up your claim that you can be the consultant your clients need. References provide a list of customers or professionals who can vouch for the quality of the work you provide in order to land new clients on a continuous basis. This list is also a starting point for your consulting work because these individuals may be willing to hire you again in the future on a project-to-project basis. Past customers can also be valuable resources for referrals for new business.

Business know-how: Becoming a consultant and running your own consulting business also requires that you have some level of knowledge on how to run a business. Not only do you have to have the acumen to work as a consultant, but you also have to be able to wear all of the hats required for running a business. The business side of consulting means having the ability to write and follow a business plan, hire a staff, run the office, pay taxes, and more. If you have never run a business before, these are things you can learn in this book right along with learning how to be a consultant.

Financial considerations

When it comes to your financial situation, there is a fine line between your personal finances and the financial aspect of running a business. Financially, you must have the cash on hand to pay for the startup and operational costs of running the business, but you also need to make sure that you have enough money to pay your living expenses while you are getting the business up and running. Remember that the majority of businesses do not start to turn a profit until after the first one or two years in business. For some businesses, it is even longer. You have to have access to a pool of money to support you financially until the business starts paying for itself and starts paying you a salary.

Financial constraints are probably the largest deterrent for individuals looking to start a career as a consultant. They may be making a satisfactory income in their current position as an employee, not have enough savings to give up this current income, or lack the ambition or motivation to shoulder the risk of starting a new business. Most business experts suggest you have enough money in cash reserves to cover your personal and business expenses for at least six months to a year.

If you do not currently have this amount of cash reserves, then you may need to save some additional money before launching your consulting business. Another option is to look to other sources such as a small business loan or borrowing money from a friend or family member to cover the costs of starting the business. Here are some ways you can prepare financially for your transition to being the owner of a consulting business:

Beef up your savings account: Start planning your consulting career by putting away as much money as possible before you jump in with both feet. Saving as much as possible provides you with a bigger safety net to cover both regular and emergency expenses. Take a look at the balance of your savings account. If you are currently living from paycheck to paycheck, now may not be the time to become a full-time consultant. If you have funds that can be easily liquidated such as stocks, bonds, mutual funds, or other assets, then you may have the safety net you need to fall back on until your business starts turning a profit.

Income and assets to cover expenses: Create a list of personal and expected business expenses, then see how many months or years the balance of cash you have will cover your expenses. Is your current after-tax income covering your current expenses? Do you have money you can pull from to cover these expenses if your income fluctuates or changes as you transition into consulting? If not, you may want to consider saving additional money or working as a part-time consultant until you can get your financial situation on steady ground. Starting a new career and business is stressful enough without having the added stress of being financially unstable. Start off financially stable so that if your consulting income is not enough to pay your expenses, you have options to fall back on until you can take on more clients, charge more for your services, or find a way to reduce your expenses.

Protect your future: Even as your business starts to take off, there are going to be financial good times and financial bad times. It is important to plan for the less-than-optimal times when you may not have enough clients or be generating enough revenue in your business to cover expenses. When times are good in your business, make sure to put away money for unexpected expenses or tougher times. For example, the mortgage industry is a very cyclical business, and as a mortgage consultant, you will need to take into account when interest rates are high because your business could slow down. If there is a large, unexpected expense, this ensures you have funds to keep your business afloat until the good times come back around again. If your office bathroom springs a leak and floods your entire office (and you do not have insurance to cover this type of catastrophe), you may have to pay to clean up the water and replace any equipment, furniture, flooring, walls, and other items damaged in the flood.

Chapter 7 goes into more detail about how to estimate your business expenses and how much you need to have to launch and keep your business afloat until it is self-sufficient. Right now, it is essential to consider where you need to start to assess whether now is the time to launch the business or if a little more preparation is in order.

Personal considerations

Starting a business, especially a consulting business, has a personal side to it. Being a consultant is a service-based business, which means you are going to be working directly with your clients, either face-to-face or by phone. It is slightly different from a product-based business where you are selling an item someone else manufactures.

On top of the personal side of business, starting a small business requires a lot of personal dedication and commitment in order to start small and grow into a larger, profit-making machine. Launching and maintaining a business can take a personal toll on you and your family. Addressing the concern that launching your consulting business may and probably is going to take time away from your personal time right now helps you to prepare and decide if a consulting business is the right choice for you.

Seek advice from others: Talk with your spouse, children, other family members, and friends to see what their opinions are on starting your business. Analyzing the launch of your consulting career from all of the different angles can help make the difference between succeeding and failing. You may also want to spend time talking with people you know who started their own businesses and even reach out to other consultants.

Personal lifestyle: If you work during the traditional office hours of 9 a.m. to 5 p.m. and have weekends off, this schedule can be turned upside down when you become a consultant. You will have clients and situations where you have to work on the weekends or field a client call at midnight on a Friday or have to leave your child's school play because there is an emergency situation you have to correct. The line between your personal life and your work life becomes blurred.

Motivation level: One of the biggest personal characteristics a consultant must possess is self-motivation. Especially when you first start your business, you may be the one and only employee. This means that there is not a manager peering over your shoulder to make sure that you are doing everything you are supposed to be doing. You have to be able to manage yourself, set your schedule, meet deadlines, juggle clients, and set and meet goals all on your own. Some people can thrive and survive in this type of environment while others need a more structured work style. You have to know yourself and assess your ability to manage yourself in order to excel in a consulting career. If you struggle with keeping yourself on task and motivated to accomplish your goals, then you may struggle starting your own business.

Is There a Need You Can Fill?

Nearly 600,000 new small businesses open each year, but that does not mean all 600,000 are going to reel in profits. According to the National Federation of Independent Business (NFIB) 39 percent of these businesses are profitable, 30 percent break even, and 30 percent lose money — 1 percent falls in the "unable to determine" category. With a multitude of mitigating factors, determining the success or failure rate of these companies, there is not a litmus test you can take to see if your business will fall in the success or failure pile. Removing everything else from the equation, you need to ask yourself one important question: Is my consulting business marketable?

One of the biggest ways to ensure success is to make sure your consulting business has a market of customers ready and willing to buy your services. No matter how great you think your idea is, if there is not an audience of paying customers to hire you then you will quickly go down in flames. Rather than try to create a market for your business, create your business to fill the need of a particular market. Think long and hard about who your potential clients are. What groups of businesses, organizations, or individuals need the consulting services you are thinking of providing? Sit down with a pen and paper in hand and create a list of broad categories of potential clients. Then start to narrow down potential clients using trade publications, phone books, the Internet, and working through your network of contacts to get more specific on who these potential clients are, how they think, where they act, and anything else you can determine about their thoughts and behaviors. When you are having conversations with people, ask them what kind of services they need that you may be able to fulfill. While they may not be able to specifically tell you the service they are looking for, you may be able to create a service based on a need you are hearing about.

Finally, do some quick competitive research. See if there are consultants out in the world offering services that fit the needs of the potential clients you have gathered information from. The truth of the matter is that there probably is at least one other consultant out there offering the service you are thinking of providing. Even if there are several consultants offering the service, there is something unique about you and your service offering that sets you apart from the competition. Determine what this innovative item is, write it down, and set it aside for now. You will need this information later when it comes time to write your business and marketing plan.

Doing work you love can be personally rewarding, but it is also important to determine if doing what you love can be profitable. While it may take one or two years for your consulting business to start turning a profit, the business has to have the ability to turn a profit in the long run in order for it to be prosperous. When researching your competition, see what the fees are that they are charging. Use these fees in conjunction with your potential client list to calculate an estimate of revenues for your business. Start out with conservative figures and estimate monthly, quarterly, and annual income. Take into consideration that the first few years are going to be slower going than later years, but put some realistic facts and figures down on paper. A good place to start is with your current income. If your current annual income is $75,000, set the goal for your first year at the same number and work backward to figure out if this is a realistic goal for the business.

Then you have to ask yourself the million-dollar question: Can the business generate enough in revenues to cover and eventually exceed expenses?

The economic turn of events

Starting in 2007 and continuing through 2010, a downturn in the economy has had a direct effect on the timing of starting a consulting business. As more and more companies are forced to close their doors or downsize, an unprecedented number of people — some highly qualified individuals — are unemployed and without many option for future employment. When times are tough, it may be next to impossible to find a company to hire you.

This is where starting a consulting business using your skills and expertise can come in handy.

Even in hard times, businesses need individuals to perform tasks that keep the business running and profitable. Hiring a consultant to perform some or all of these tasks can be a highly cost effective option for companies to utilize. For example, one of the first departments to get cutbacks or axed altogether in a company is typically the marketing department. The challenge companies face is that they can no longer to keep the marketing professionals on staff, but they also cannot afford to give up on their marketing efforts altogether either. If you have years of experience in marketing, you can fill the need these companies have by becoming the marketing arm of their business and they save money because they are paying you on a per-project basis rather than paying your salary, health insurance, retirement account, and all of the other costs associated with having a full-time employee.

So even though the job market itself may look bleak with companies cutting back budgets, laying off employees, or closing their doors forever, these situations may create opportunities for consulting businesses making it a prime time to get your business up and running. On the other hand, more stringent lending guidelines have made it harder for individuals and small businesses to obtain new credit and loans. This means that it may be difficult for you to borrow or find the seed money you need to pay for your startup costs, making it more important than ever to make sure you have your finances in order before you decide to start your consulting firm.

Self-assessment Test

Now that you have some foundational information on considerations for starting your consulting business, it is time to take a short test to assess whether consulting is up your alley and if it is right time to take that leap. While there are not any right and wrong answers to the test, answering the questions helps you determine what areas you may need to work on before launching your new company.

Choose the most appropriate answer for each question. Answer honestly and only choose one answer for each question. Mark the answer you choose so you can tally your score and evaluate your responses at the end of the test. You may want to have a calculator on hand to add up your score.

1. Are you a problem solver?

   a. Solving problems is what I live to do.
   b. I enjoy solving certain types of problems.
   c. I will trade you one of my problems for one of your problems.
   d. There must be someone else who can solve this problem.
   e. I cannot stand solving problems.

2. Are setting and completing goals up your alley?

   a. Absolutely.

    b.   I am good at setting goals but not so great at reaching them.

    c.   I am willing to learn how to set and reach goals.

    d.   My goals set themselves.

    e.   I do not have any goals.

3.   Are you self-motivated?

    a.   I get up in the morning with my "to do" list in hand, ready to get started.

    b.   While I can work independently, I sometimes have a hard time getting started.

    c.   I want to work on my own but have always had someone to tell me what to do when it comes to work.

    d.   Tell me what I need to do to be a self-starter and I can probably learn how to do it.

    e.   Who, me?

4.   How would you rate your work style confidence?

    a.   I get the job done no matter what.

    b.   I usually get the job done.

    c.   I am not sure if I can get the job done.

    d.   I never get the job done.

    e.   What job?

5.   Do you enjoy hurdling over obstacles in order to complete your tasks?

    a.   Persistence is my middle name.

    b.   Most of the time I do, but sometimes I avoid difficult problems.

    c.   No one is perfect and neither am I.

    d.   Is my work ever done?

    e.   Some things are better left undone.

6.   Are you adaptable to change?

    a.   Change is my game.

    b.   I can change if I feel it is necessary, but I am uncomfortable with unnecessary changes.

    c.   Change happens no matter what.

    d.   As long as I am not the one that has to change.

    e.   I am a creature of habit.

7.   How do you rate your creativity?

    a.   Give me five minutes, and I will have a list of solutions for your problem.

    b.   It depends on my mood.

    c.   Can I have some time to mull that question over?

    d.   I should not have to reinvent the wheel.

    e.   What's wrong with the way things are?

8.   Are you a people person?

    a.   The people part of work is what makes it good.

    b.   It depends on the people we are talking about.

    c.   I like to work with people as opposed to animals.

    d.   I am more of the solo type.

    e.   Me, myself, and I.

9.   Trustworthy, loyal, honest, and brave are adjectives used to describe you.

    a.   Yes.

    b.   Three-quarters of them, yes. One-quarter, no.

    c.   50/50.

    d.   Other adjectives are used.

    e.   Is this the last question of the test?

10. How important is making money to you?

    a.   I feel there is no limit on how much money I can make.

    b.   Work less, earn more is my motto.

    c.   I live comfortably.

    d.   I do not even know what enough money is.

    e.   I keep playing the lottery.

Tally Your Score

> Each A answer = 5 points
> Each B answer = 3 points
> Each C answer = 0 points
> Each D answer = -3 points
> Each E answer = -5 points

Now it is time to see where you stand. Add and subtract all of your points based on the scale about for your final score.

More than 50 points or less than -50 points: Make sure your calculator is working properly. If you used a paper and pencil and did the math in your head, you better use the calculator to tally your score this time.

-25 to -50 points: Consulting is not the career move for you. Stop reading this book right now and pass it along to someone who has the potential to score higher than you did.

-1 to -24 points: Consulting is not really up your alley at the moment. You should continue to read this book though to learn more about consulting. When you finish reading, retake the test to see if you score higher.

0 points: You are on the fence between being an employee and launching your consulting career. Continue to research the field of consulting, read this book thoroughly, and revisit the test and the possibility of consulting in a couple of months.

1 to 24 points: You have consulting potential and should consider starting your consulting career in the near future. While starting out, you may want to continue with your full-time day job until you get the business up, running, and self-sufficient. Use this book as your guide to streamline the process of starting and running a successful consulting business.

25 to 50 points: When they made the consultant mold, they used you as the model. If you are not already a consultant, it is time to get your business going and quit your day job. While you have the skill set to make it happen in a big way, use this book to hone your skills and cement your level of success.

☐ Checklist
☐ List your reason(s) for wanting to turn into a consultant.
☐ Analyze the personal, professional, and financial considerations of starting and running a consulting business and make sure everything is in order.
☐ Take and score the self-assessment test and determine if consulting is the right career for you.

Chapter 2

What Type of Consultant Are You?

In this chapter, you will:

- Decide what type of consultant you want to be.

- Assess your personal and financial situation in order to help you make your consulting type choice.

- Discover the various types of consultants and some of the industries consultants serve.

- See what consultants do (services, products, and advice they offer clients).

- Observe a "day-in-the-life" look of what being a consultant looks like.

- Learn some of the pitfalls a consultant faces when working with clients.

- Learn suggestions on how to avoid making these same mistakes.

Now that you know consulting is the right career move for you, it is time to start dealing with the details of becoming a consultant. Consulting is not a one-size-fits-all career. It is a career position that has some flexibility built into it as far as how to set it up. Some consultants operate their business on the side while they continue to work a full-time job. Others solely have the intention of working as a consultant on a part-time basis in order to earn additional income. The final set of consultants operate on a full-time basis where consulting is their only line of work and main source of income.

How you establish and run your consulting business has everything to do with your personal, professional, and financial situation. For example, if you are the sole breadwinner and provider for your family, it may not be a viable option to quit your day job right now and launch a new business. Instead, it may be a better option to continue working full time while you run your consulting business on the side. As your business grows and you start turning a profit adequate enough to cover your personal and business expenses, then you can transition into consulting full time.

Another popular option for those who wish to work as a consultant but are not yet ready to launch their own business is to land a consulting position with an established consulting firm. This allows you to work in the consulting field, enjoy some of the flexibility of working as a consultant, and to earn the income a consultant can pull in without having the headache of being a business owner at the same time. Working for a consulting firm has its advantages because you typically earn a salary and receive employee benefits such as health insurance and a retirement plan.

You may also benefit because there is a set of established clients for you to work with or you may be expected to find your own clients. Especially if you have not worked as a consultant before, working for an established firm may set the stage for you to go out on your own later. You can learn a lot from working for a consulting firm — skills and ideas that you can modify and use to launch your own business when the time is right. Rather than going from zero to 60, you can take a slower and more direct route to opening your own consulting business.

Consultant Industries

One of the best things about choosing a career as a consultant is you can consult on almost anything for any type of consumer, business, or organization. When people think of consultants, they generally think of those that service for-profit companies, but there are consultants that service consumers, for-profit and nonprofit companies and organizations, government agencies, schools, and more.

While some consultants cater to a particular type of business entity, most choose to narrow their service offering down even further. Some consultants provide services to a particular department, such as the finance department, the operations area, or the marketing department. Other types of consultants limit their services to a particular industry. How specific a consultant gets is up to them: You may find a consultant who specializes in personal finance companies that cater to professional women in the state of Florida. The more highly specialized a consultant is, the smaller the pool of potential clients usually is. On the flip side, the more highly specialized a consultant is, the higher the fee typically is for the consultant's services because clients with a specific need are willing to pay a premium to work with a consultant with the experience that fits that need.

When it comes down to it, a consultant can be involved in almost any type of business. Tasks for consultants can range from writing reports based on studies the consultant has conducted to developing and delivering training to creating and implementing designs. There are consultants who simply evaluate company organizational structures and make recommendations to the company on how they can go about streamlining jobs and processes to make it more efficient. Then there are consultants responsible for creating building layouts for individuals or businesses so that the occupants of the building get the most use of the space. Again, it all comes down to two things. First, it is about how your expertise is valuable to your clients. Second, it is about fulfilling a need that exists in the market. The consultant's job is to determine what the problem is, handle the company's need, and satisfy the need quickly, inexpensively and effectively.

You may look at various types of companies and wonder why consultants are not on the company payroll, at least as an outsourcing option. Many businesses are working with consultants, but it may not be visible or obvious to the outside world. Generally, businesses hire consultants for almost any need. You will find consultants working with different types of organizations on anything from professional office organization to establishing and implementing advertising campaigns. Some consultants choose to specialize in one specific aspect, while other consultants provide all of the services that fall under their realm. Here are some examples of specialized consulting:

- **Advertising:** Create and execute advertising campaigns and materials (online and off); organize and manage the advertising budget; obtain and manage sponsorships.

- **Computers:** Evaluate company computer and technology needs; help clients make purchases; set up networks, programs, programming, and perform maintenance; Web design services and website content creation.

- **Health care:** Work with hospitals for patient needs; patient record management; update computer files; work with individual patients to manage their needs; develop cost-savings plan for the hospitals and health organizations.

As you can see, the list can be extensive with consultants performing a wide variety of tasks, large and small, based on their skills. While you may think being more of a generalist when it comes to consulting is better, many businesses prefer to work with someone who is a specialist. When you specialize in a certain area, you are positioned as an expert in your field, become a valuable commodity to the client, and can warrant a higher fee because clients are willing to pay more for top performers like you.

Franchise consulting

Another option for starting your consulting business is to buy a franchise. The benefit of buying into a consulting franchise is that you essentially buy a "turnkey" business, where all of the plans are built for you and all you have to do is follow the plan to run the business. Franchises have an established business model and provide you with all of the support you need to make the consulting business a successful venture. The problem is that franchise companies have strict sets of rules, which leaves little room for your own creativity. The cost of investing in a franchise can be another drawback because the franchise has set fees and costs involved in buying into one.

For example, if you buy a 360 Solutions (**www.360solutions. com**) franchise, you are buying an established business model for running a business. Not only does this franchise offer a business manual you can follow as a guide to run your business, but buying into the franchise also comes with a branding strategy, website, e-mail, and private label. When you invest money in a franchise, you are investing money in training, materials, and the guidelines you need to follow to run a successful consulting business. Because the business methodology is established, when you open a consulting franchise, you lower your chance of failure as opposed to if you start a consulting business from scratch. Investing in a consulting franchise can help you to avoid making mistakes that can cost a great deal of time and money, which can put your investment at risk for a partial or complete loss.

As is the case with starting any business, buying into a consulting franchise requires an up-front investment. Up-front investment costs may be as small as a few thousand dollars and can go up to hundreds of thousands of dollars — all depending on the franchise. For example, to buy a 360 Solutions franchise, the total investment ranges from $9,500 to $55,000. Some franchisors offer financing options so you can finance the purchase and operating expenses of owning and operating the franchise by making monthly payments. When you buy into a franchise, your financial obligations do not end with the purchase. Franchises typically require you to pay an annual fee for using the name, and some even require you to pay a percentage of the profits.

For more information on franchises, the Small Business Administration (SBA) website (**www.sba.gov**) offers a "Is Franchising for Me?" workbook. When you go to the SBA website, click on the Small Business Planner tab to access the guide. Franchise Gator (**www.franchisegator.com**), a company that boasts the largest directory of business opportunities and franchises online, also lists franchise opportunities by investment level and industry.

The Role of a Consultant

In some way, shape, or form, the business of consulting has been around for hundreds of decades. While some the earliest consultants had to forge their own way and find the path to their own successes, these pioneers have since paved the way for the consultants that have come behind them. Whether you are a self-employed consultant or a consultant working for a consulting firm, the role of a consultant comes down to a succinct and simple five-step process.

There are a lot of little tasks and sub-roles that fall into each of the five steps, but these steps cover the five major roles a consultant fulfills for its clients.

Step 1: Determining and defining a problem:

Clients hire consultants to help the clients identify an issue or problem that exists within the organization. For example, a manufacturing company may know its production time is too long, but it may not know what is causing it or how to correct it. A consultant can evaluate the production process and determine what is causing the delay in production.

Step 2: Data collection:

As a third-party source of information, a consultant brought into a company or organization collects data surrounding the problem or issue that the organization is facing. This helps the consultant determine what may be causing the problem or issue to occur. In the manufacturing example, the consultant may review reports and meet with management and other members of the company to uncover what may have changed from the time production levels were high to when production levels dropped.

Step 3: Solving the problem:

Once a consultant identifies the problem and collects the data that reveals what the problem is, the consultant is then responsible for solving the problem. If the consultant determines that a change in the manufacturing process is what has caused the production levels to dip, the consultant may map out a streamlined process the company can follow to bring production levels back to the optimum level. Typically, a consultant will come up with several different options for the client to use to resolve the issue.

Step 4: Make recommendations:

The consultant is then responsible for presenting his or her recommendations to the client. Because you are an expert, the advice given to the client is based on your experience, expertise, evaluations, and data collection for each client. Generally, the consultant presents each of the solutions the client can use to resolve the problem and guides the client into choosing the option that best fits the client's needs. The presentation includes the advantages and disadvantages to the client for each option so the client can make an educated decision about which option it should implement to get rid of the problem.

Step 5: Implement the recommendation:

Finally, the consultant typically walks the client through the process of implementing the chosen recommendation. Again, because the consultant is an expert, it helps the client to resolve their problem faster and easier when the consultant is involved with the process from the beginning and follows it through to the end.

This five-step method applies to any type of consultant regardless of the industry you serve. This method can help clients find answers to the questions they have.

Even when you specialize in a particular area, consulting work has some tasks and roles that are universal. The part that consultants play when interacting with clients is what makes the consultant valuable to the clients. Because you are working with the companies as an independent contractor and not an employee, if you do not provide them with the best service then they will turn to someone else for the service you are providing. As a consultant, this means you lose a client, thus losing money and the potential for future and referral business from that client. If you provide poor quality work as an employee, you may get fired and have to find another job, but when you own a business, shoddy work can crumble the entire foundation, putting you out of business quickly. Therefore, when reading through what a consultant does, think about how you can keep your own clients satisfied and ready to work with you repeatedly.

To Do: Listen to their needs

From the time you are wooing a prospective client to the time you sign them as a client, all of your interactions with the company and its representatives comes down to determining what the company needs are. In fact, this may be the most important part of consulting work because this analysis permits you to determine which of the services you provide will fit the client's needs. Determining and understanding the client's needs allows you to create a proposal that leaves the client understanding what you offer and how you can help them fulfill their needs.

Listening is one of the primary skills allowing consultants to gather as much information about a company as possible before spewing out potential solutions to the client. Listening and taking in as much information as possible allows you to garner a big picture view of the problem and position your services as a resolution in a confident, educated, and qualified manner.

To Do: Gather more details

Even when you think you have all of the information, the odds are good that there is still information you are missing. Your job as a consultant is to act as a type of investigator where you are constantly searching for and uncovering more details and more information. As a consultant, you must fully understand the situation the client is in before you try to fix it. For example, if you are a computer networking consultant and you are working with a client that has a malfunctioning computer system, your first instinct may be to start pulling apart the network to uncover the problem. Rather than jump right into breaking the system down, you need to thoroughly investigate what the whole problem is and why it is happening. The only true way to do this is to gather additional information from the client and each employee that is experiencing a problem from the computer network. This permits you to fully grasp what the problem is so you can make informed decisions on what needs to get done.

To Do: Analyze the components

Once you have the necessary information, your next task is to analyze all of the information you have gathered. This is the portion of your role where you ask yourself what is causing the problem to occur in the first place. Similar to a doctor considering a patient's symptoms and lifestyle before making a diagnosis, consulting work requires you to find out the symptoms before making a diagnosis as well. By reviewing the symptoms, a consultant is able to see how everything links together.

For example, if you are working with a business that is struggling financially, you may be brought on as a consultant to determine what is causing the financial troubles, so you can implement the changes necessary to make it profitable again. In order to do this, you have to talk to the employee or individual who is managing the profit and loss statement for the business. If he or she shows you that company revenues have dropped 10 percent over the past six months, this is simply a symptom of the problem.

A day in the life of a consultant

When you interview for a job, one of the first questions you should ask is, "What does a day in the life of this position look like?" Getting a visual view of what your daily routine will be like as a consultant can help you envision whether it is a position you are going to like or one you may end up loathing.

Your days may look slightly different when you first get started because you will have some startup tasks to get the business off the ground. Once you get the business up and running, you will have more time to focus on obtaining new clients and servicing the clients you already have.

Another thing to take into consideration is that when you first start your consulting business, you will probably be the only employee. When you are the only worker, this means you wear all of the hats for the running the business — from cleaning the office bathroom and answering the phone to working on client projects and conducting the marketing tasks. As your business grows and starts to make some money, you can start to delegate some of these duties so that you can focus solely on the moneymaking tasks of the business, which is working on client projects.

Now that all of the disclaimers are out of the way, this is how a consultant's daily schedule may look:

Time	To Do:
8 a.m. - 9 a.m.	Check and respond to e-mails and phone messages
9 a.m. - 10 a.m.	Conduct online research for current client projects

10 a.m. - 11 a.m.	Make phone calls to speak to parties that have information for client project
11 a.m. - noon	Prepare written report of your Internet and phone research
Noon - 12:30 p.m.	Lunch
12:30 p.m. - 1 p.m.	Check and respond to e-mails and phone messages
1 p.m. - 1:30 p.m.	Travel to client meeting
2 p.m. - 3 p.m.	Meeting with a prospective client at their office
3 p.m. - 3:30 p.m.	Travel back to the office
3:30 p.m. - 4 p.m.	Prepare and send follow-up e-mail and proposal to prospective client you met
4 p.m. - 5 p.m.	Marketing tasks: Cold calling, postcard, letter, or e-mail to prospective clients
5 p.m. - 6 p.m.	Prepare to-do list and schedule for tomorrow

Time management

Managing your time wisely is a skill you can learn (if you do not possess it already). As is the case with almost any goal or objective, keeping a written or electronic schedule can help to keep you on track every day. Prepare the next day's schedule the night before will allow you to hit the ground running each morning when you arrive at your office — whether you simply walk into the guest bedroom of your house that has been transformed into your office or you rent an office space a few miles away from your home.

The sample schedule breaks the consultant's day into 30- and 60-minute segments. You may feel comfortable with these time frames, or you may choose to break your day into shorter or longer segments. For example, some consultants choose to focus on client projects in chunks of two-hour periods and only dedicate 30 minutes at a time to marketing, administrative tasks, and other tasks. While your daily schedule will look slightly different, there are some tasks that need to be on your schedule every day: responding to e-mails and phone calls, marketing your business, and working on client projects need to be addressed every day no matter what else you accomplish. While you may be receiving e-mails all day (and you probably will be), try to focus your time reading and responding to these e-mails during your scheduled time. Reading and responding to e-mails can quickly distract you from the productive activities you should be focusing on. Before you know it, you have lost hours of time you should have been focusing on making money. There will also be days when you are out of the office all day visiting a client site to observe, gather data, or share findings with the client on their project. Even on days where you are out of the office all day long, you want to schedule a short segment of time for responding to e-mails and phone messages as well as performing at least one marketing effort such as sending out a referral request letter to past clients or an e-mail announcement of a new service you are offering.

The Common Consulting Pitfalls

While the majority of this book covers how to become the best consultant you can be, there are just as many things you do not want to do in order to be a successful consultant. Change is a scary element for most people, and the employees and owners of a business you are working with as a consultant are no exceptions to this rule. When a consultant comes along, assesses the company problems, and wants to make changes to the way things are done, the delicate balance of the company is shaken, which means you may feel resistance in your advice and implementing your recommendations. The most important thing to remember is that, if done in the right way, you can communicate virtually anything you need to in order to urge someone who truly wants change for the better within the organization. On the other hand, if someone resists, there may be nothing you can say to make him or her accept and implement the change.

Arrogance can cost you in more ways than one

Arrogance should be removed from your demeanor and is one of the key things to avoid when working as a consultant. You may have the best and most relevant experience and information to move the company to the next level in its industry, but if you come across as arrogant, it may create a lack of belief in you and your methodologies, meaning the client may not hire you. However, do not confuse arrogance with confidence because you should present yourself as someone who knows what you are doing but not to the point where it is all about you instead of being all about the client. As a consultant, you want to fully support the organization and carefully communicate your recommendations in a diplomatic manner — without stepping on any toes.

For example, if you determine the company's current website is not turning a profit because it has too many banners that are distracting customers, you need to present this determination to the group of owners and managers who have designed the website in a cautious manner. It comes down to the old adage you probably heard your mother say a million times: "It is not about what you say but how you say it." If you say, "Your Web designer should have known better than to put these horrible banners on the site. Anyone who has basic knowledge of Web design knows this distracts customers and can cause a loss in sales," then all you may be left with is an angry and offended client. Not only have you told the company and its employees that they lack basic Web design knowledge, but you also have insulted those who will likely have to make the changes you are suggesting.

Using a more tactful approach can prevent insult and help you stay on the good side of your client so they will be more likely to heed your advice. Try saying this instead: "I have taken the time to explore the website, and I have some specific recommendations for you. First, we should reconsider the flash banners on the front page. While other websites use these types of banners, I feel that they are obtrusive to your goals because they are distracting to the visitors to the site. I have a few ideas that we can work together on for different methods of advertising that have proven to be more effective in boosting sales."

The same message is stated but in two different manners, the latter being far less confrontational and involves everyone in the solution to the problem than the former.

Keeping clients in the dark

Open and two-way communication is the key element of any successful relationship. In order to build successful relationships with your clients, you have to communicate both the good and the bad points. This may include telling the client his or her ideas are wrong or are not working toward helping the company accomplish its goals. If you do not tell your clients everything they need to know from the beginning and throughout the process or if you hide any of the facts, it is more likely that you and your client will fail rather than succeed. *Chapter 11 provides some specific instructions on how to deliver this news to the client in a professional and productive manner.*

There also may be some uncomfortable times when a recommendation you have implemented is not working. Rather than hide this from the client, be proactive and address problems as they arise, always keeping the business owner or managers of the company in the loop. Delivering bad news or admitting that you were not right is only uncomfortable for a moment, but it is far better than keeping up the charade and making the problem worse.

Going overboard

When you work as a consultant, it is important to stay on task and focus on the job you were hired to do. This does not in any way mean you should not go above and beyond for your client, but it does mean not to create work that the client does not necessarily need in order to pad your own pockets. The best way to get repeat work and referral business from an existing client is do the best work you can with the work at hand. If you create a new problem in an effort to garner more work from the client, you are going to have a hard time showing how you add value to the company at the end of the project because the project was not a legitimate problem.

For example, the sales at a local retail store are dropping, and they hire you to help them determine what is causing the problem and make suggestions on how to resolve the issue. You determine that the loss of sales is due to a competitor that opened a location down the street. Under your contract with the retail store, you are reviewing a new marketing campaign they are about to roll out. Instead of focusing your efforts on the marketing campaign at hand, you encourage the company to rearrange the layout of the store, which allows you to incorporate a higher fee for your services and incur a larger profit for you. The intention and implementation of the recommendation does not help the company increase its sales; it is a waste of the client's time and money. While the client may believe in your recommendation, when they do not see the results later, they may see the recommendation for what it really is, which can jeopardize the relationship with the client and eliminate the possibility of referrals from the client for future business.

Making promises you cannot keep

Many consultants make the mistake of promising a client they can do something that is impossible to deliver or the consultant does not have the ability to do. Most of the time this is done in an effort to please the client, but if the task is not something that is under your scope of knowledge or is simply too much for you to handle, let the client know this. Do not make the assumption that the company wants you to do everything for them. Give your honest recommendations to the company but realize that you are only human and the client is going to respect you a lot more for your honesty.

Many consultants take on jobs they are not experts in with the hope of becoming experts through the learning experience. This may seem like you are being helpful to the client, but rather than help the client, it may simply leave a bad impression of you and your services. This can cause you to lose the client and the revenue you derive from working with them, as well as put future client referrals in jeopardy. If the work the client is requesting or that you are recommending is beyond what you can comfortably complete, do not push yourself into the role of the implementer. Instead, only make recommendations that you can do without failing or refer the proper person or organization to complete the task at hand. Do not take on more than you can successfully complete on your own. Likewise, it is also important to keep all of the promises you make. If you tell a client you are going to do something, then in order to uphold your professional reputation and integrity, you better do it.

For example, if your client proposal includes an investment of eight hours a day on your part, then you are likely dedicating all of your time to that company project. Do not promise the client you will do ten hours of work in eight hours, unless you have every intention of working ten hours a day. Also, do not promise to do more work than what the budget allows for either. Over-promising can cause you to under-deliver when it comes to the quality of the work you provide to the business, which only hurts you and your business in the process.

Paying attention to the wrong people

As you are working on client projects, you may find yourself in contact with and getting on the radar screen of other companies or individuals who need your services. It may be tempting to meet with them and work through their needs as a new prospective client while putting your current client on hold. This may seem like a primary way to create additional work for you and your business, but it may be at the cost of your consultant career.

If you have allotted time to your current client projects, make sure that you are using the time to focus on their projects. Avoid neglecting your current customers with the hope of landing new ones. If you do not provide high-quality service to your current clients, chances are good that you may lose the client altogether, which means you are unable to count on the client for their revenue. At the same time, it may frustrate the new client because you do not have enough time to invest in the project. In the end, you end up hurting three companies: your company and both client companies.

Simply schedule a time to meet with the prospective client outside of the time set aside for the current client. Once you sign the new client, you can adjust your daily schedule to dedicate time to each client project fairly based on their needs. Set deadlines and expectations with the client while keeping your total workload in mind. This allows you to provide dedicated and quality service to all of your clients rather than sacrificing one client for another client. *Chapter 8 covers more on refining your time management skills so that you can juggle clients without sacrificing quality for quantity.*

☐ **Checklist**
☐ Assess whether your personal and financial situation affects what type of consulting you can accomplish.
☐ Decide what types of companies you can serve and narrow it down by industry and region, if applicable.
☐ Decide which services, products, and advice you want to offer your clients.
☐ See if you can carry out the role of a consultant based on the "day-in-the-life" look of a consultant.
☐ Recognize and avoid making some of the common mistakes when working with clients.

Chapter 3

Planning a Successful Leap into Consulting

In this chapter, you will:

- Discover the pros and cons of setting up a home office or renting an office space.

- Learn how to set up your home office or rent office space.

- Gather information on office furniture, equipment, and other business essentials you need to get your office ready for work.

- Uncover how to line up professional help and support for your business.

Even if you have consulting experience, setting up your own consulting office can present a challenge. If you have chosen to work as a consultant for an established firm, then your office space options are probably decided for you. Otherwise, your first decision when setting up your own consulting company is whether you want to run the business from your home or you need to rent office space. As is the case with almost every decision you make in the business world and in life, there are pros and cons to establishing a home-based office and in setting up an office outside the home.

Consulting is different from being a manicurist or florist. While manicurists and florists have clients come to their shops, this is not typically the case with consulting work. In fact, if anything, the opposite is true. Most consultants perform their work in their own space and visit the clients' locations for any projects. With this in mind, most consultants choose the cost effectiveness and convenience of running their consulting business out of their home rather than renting an office space. Three other choices generally exist for establishing a consulting business space: rent an office space, use a flextime office rental space, or share a space.

The Home Office

Opening your consulting business as a home-based business may be the most logical choice when it comes to financing your endeavor. After all, if you are already paying rent or paying your mortgage then it does not cost you any additional money to set up your home office. Two key elements you need to keep in mind when deciding if a home office is the right setup for you are determining if you have space in your home for an office and whether your home provides enough privacy for you to conduct business.

The first thing you need to consider is whether you have space in your home to establish and operate your consulting business. If you live alone in a one- or two-bedroom apartment, then you can set up your business in the corner of your dining room or in the extra bedroom. If you have a family, then you need to make sure you have a room in the house where you can shut out the rest of the world for peace and quiet when it is time to talk to a client on the phone or concentrate on your work. Generally, to run a consulting business, you only need an office that is large enough to hold your desk, chair, computer, printer, and phone. Most consultants do not meet face-to-face with clients in the consultant's office, so it is not usually necessary to have extra space for holding client meetings or welcoming prospective clients into your office.

Consulting will either be your part-time or full-time income earner, so it is important to treat your career seriously. If your home office is the home dining room table that you have to clear every night so your family can eat dinner, then the situation is probably not conducive to running your business and serving as your office. Spare bedrooms, a den, a garage, the attic, or a finished basement are all viable options for a home office. This allows you to dedicate the space you need to your work environment and you can leave your work one night and come back to it and pick up right where you left off undisturbed the next morning.

Kids, spouses, and pets may all be wonderful things to surround yourself with, but these same wonderments can be a hindrance when you are trying to run your consulting business. During your home office evaluation stage, be sure to evaluate if the space you are considering for your office offers enough privacy for you to get your work done, make phone calls, and talk with clients without interruptions. For example, setting up your office on the kitchen table or in a corner of your living room where you cannot shut out the rest of the house noise during business hours can end up being more of a hindrance to getting your work done than a private area with a door.

The IRS allows you to write off a space in your home that has full-time office status. For example, if your home office takes up 10 percent of the total square footage of your home, then you are able to write off 10 percent of your mortgage (principal and interest) or rent amount. This can offer a significant tax deduction, but the entire room has to be dedicated to your business in order for you to deduct it on your federal tax returns.

The Pros	The Cons
Saves you from having to pay rent for an office	Blurs the line between your personal and business life
Convenient because you do not have to commute	Is not conducive for times when you need to have face-to-face meetings
Saves time because you do not have to commute	Requires installing additional phone lines and uses space in the home for business purposes
Provides a federal tax deduction when you have dedicated space for your office in your home	

☐ Home Office **Checklist**

☐	Assess whether your personal and financial situation affects what type of consulting you can accomplish.
☐	Decide what types of companies you can serve and narrow it down by industry and region, if applicable.
☐	Decide which services, products, and advice you want to offer your clients.
☐	See if you can carry out the role of a consultant based on the "day-in-the-life" look of a consultant.
☐	Recognize and avoid making some of the common mistakes when working with clients.

Flextime Office Space

In most medium and large cities, there are flextime office space or shared rental space as an option for setting up your consulting business, which can typically be found in the yellow pages of your local phone book. Some flextime offices have "flex" in the name, but others use the term "executive" in the listing name. Shared space options allow you to rent a cubicle or office for a monthly fee. In addition to having your own dedicated workspace, these facilities also offer a receptionist to answer your business calls and forward the calls to you wherever you are or to take a message if you are unavailable. Generally, shared space options also provide limited administrative support to help you with tasks such as making copies, sending faxes, and creating correspondence. The flex space also provides you with a business mailing address where clients can send mail and packages, and there will always be someone there to sign for and accept it on your behalf.

For all intents and purposes, a flextime office space provides your business with a professional façade. Rather than answering your own phone, a receptionist answers it for you. If for some reason you do have to conduct a face-to-face meeting, you have a professional environment in which to conduct the meeting. It also provides a place to go to every day to complete your work, which some people need to get motivated and take care of business. Some flextime offices also allow renters to obtain space on an as-needed basis. Rather than pay a monthly fee for a dedicated space, you may have the option to use the facilities when and if you need them. You may opt for the mail and receptionist services to give off a professional appearance to clients and prospective clients calling your office. This option permits you to book office space or a conference room if and when you need it.

The Pros	The Cons
Provides a professional front	Costs can range from a couple hundred to $1,000 a month
Includes office furniture and supplies	There may be limitations on the personal items you can leave behind because the space is shared by other tenants
Offers some administrative support	The space has office hours so if you are inspired at midnight to work, you probably are not going to be able to access the building
Offers a dedicated work space in a professional environment	
Reduces the cost of having to rent an entire office on your own	
Reduces the cost of having to hire staff such as a receptionist or administrative support	

☐ Flextime Office Space **Checklist**

☐	What space is available to you?
☐	What office equipment is included?
☐	Do you have to pay a monthly fee, or can you on an as-needed basis?
☐	Is there a dedicated phone line for your business? If yes, does your fee payment include someone to answer the line, take messages, and transfer the calls to you?
☐	Do you have storage space for files and supplies?

Shared Office Space

Along similar lines as flex office space, you may also consider sharing office space with another professional such as an accountant or attorney. Many professional service firms rent and occupy office space that is too large for their immediate needs, leaving empty office space unused. At times, these types of professionals have extra space in their offices that they are willing to rent out. You may be able to land your own office inside one of these offices or buildings at a reduced rate. Depending on your negotiations with the professional you are renting the space from, you may even be able to use his or her receptionist and administrative support services.

The Pros	The Cons
Provides a professional environment at a reduced rate to renting your own office	You have to commute to work
Allows you to separate your business and personal life	Using shared items such as the fax machine and the sign on the office has the name of the firm you are renting from rather than your business name
Depending on the type of firm you rent from, it may be a referral source of business for you	Creates a rental payment that you would not have with a home office

☐ Shared Office Space **Checklist**

☐	What space is available to you?
☐	What office equipment is included (desk, computer, printer, and phone)?
☐	What is the monthly payment?

	Is there a dedicated phone number for your business? If yes, does your rent include someone to answer the line, take messages, and transfer the calls to you?
☐	
☐	Can you place a business sign outside the office door or on the building?

CASE STUDY: THE BENEFITS OF SHARED OFFICE SPACE

Career Momentum
Rhonda C. Messinger, M.A., G.C.D.F.
Portage, MI 49024
269-324-2003
www.careermomentum.net

Rhonda C. Messinger grew her consulting firm, Career Momentum, from a past consulting business that she owned. Although it was not the core of her business, she would help clients from time to time find careers and make career transitions. After spending time learning more about career consulting, and with encouragement from the others she had helped, she brought her services to the public. Hence, Career Momentum was born.

Messinger assists the unemployed, underemployed, and unhappily employed in finding careers that help balance their personal and professional lives. Career changes may include lateral moves in their field, moving up in their field, moving into a new field, and starting a business. She started her consulting business in her home and sometimes worked out of coffee shops. She found that it was difficult discussing confidential information in public places and even had some interesting experiences with people listening in on her conversation. Some eavesdroppers even decided to add to the conversation — that is when Messinger knew it was time to rent office space.

Messinger now shares space with another professional, which makes it more economical. Each has their own business, but the business types complement each other, which allows clients to use both services if they so desire. The main benefit of renting office space for Messinger is that her client meetings are confidential. The space also lends itself well for her to use more techniques to help clients. For example, she now videotapes clients during mock interviews and then views them with the clients in the office. Without family interruptions, Messinger can prepare for meetings and keep client information more confidential and secure.

The main disadvantage Messinger feels is that it is often lonely being an independent consultant. After she sold her last business, she swore she would not open another business again because she really missed the growth and camaraderie gained from working with others. Sharing office space with another professional helps make it a less lonely venture. Also, the cost of renting space means Messinger has to charge her clients more for services than she would like. Right now, she is below the national average for her fees, but she is not going to be able to stay there much longer and continue to be profitable.

Formal and Professional Office

The final option for setting up your consulting business is to rent, lease, or buy an office space in an existing building or as a stand-alone building. Options for obtaining a formal office space can range from renting an office condo, floor, or office space in an office building to obtaining a retail space occupied by other stores and professionals such as real estate and insurance agents. This gives you the option to pair your businesses and gain more exposure. For example, if you are opening a wedding consulting business, you may want to consider opening an office near other wedding-related businesses such as a photographer, cake bakery, florist, or limousine company. Because you all have the same audience, you have a better chance of landing business when a bride comes to meet with the photographer and sees your consulting business in the same office complex or retail center. Because the majority of these options come completely unfurnished and without any type of support staff, you will have to furnish the office and hire staff as needed. The primary disadvantage to having a formal office is all of the costs involved in setting the office up and maintaining the upkeep.

Costs

Some of the costs you need to consider before deciding on a formal office space include:

- Up-front costs and down payment of a mortgage, lease, or rental payment (a percentage of the purchase price or first, last, and current month's rent payment)

- Insurance costs for keeping the office (liability, fire, theft)

- Installing phone lines

- Purchasing furniture, equipment, and office decorations

- Alarm system and locks

- Employing administrative staff

- Housekeeping/cleaning services

- Amenities such as a fridge, coffeemaker, and microwave

The Pros	The Cons
Provides a professional work environment	Distractions such as package deliveries, the cleaning crew, and your administrative staff
Gives your business further exposure	More expensive than any other office option available

☐ Formal Office Space **Checklist**	
☐	What else does the rental space include (water, utilities)?
☐	What is the monthly payment?

☐	On top of the rental payment, what is it going to cost for electricity, phone service, cleaning, staffing, and other expenses?
☐	Will you need to hire staff to help run the office? If yes, how much will this cost for salary and benefits?
☐	Can you place a business sign outside the office door or on the building?
☐	Is the office a short commute from your home?
☐	Is the office conveniently located for business meetings with clients and vendors?
☐	Is the office located near related businesses that may be a referral source for business?

Furniture, Equipment, and other Business Essentials

Whether you decide to establish your consulting business in a home office or rent an office space, you next step is determining the furniture, business equipment, and other supplies you need to get your business up and running and operating on a daily basis. These are the minimal necessities you need to get started. As your business continues to grow, your needs may, and probably will, change.

Phone

The primary business tool you need for your consulting business is probably a telephone. You should have a dedicated phone number for your business, especially if you are working from a home office. The last thing you want is a client calling in the middle of dinner or in the middle of the night and disrupting your personal family time. You may wish to have a telephone with at least two lines or at a very minimum have one phone line with call-waiting service. It is very unprofessional for a client to call your office and receive a busy signal, so you want to make sure that even if you are on the phone your clients can still get through to you. Along the same lines, you also want to have voice mail service connected to your business phone. Voice mail helps to capture calls from clients when you are not in the office, but it also helps you to capture client messages when you are on the other line or do not make it to the phone in time to answer their call.

Because a consultant is often out of the office and traveling to and from client locations, you also need to have a reliable cell phone or smart phone to use for your business. You may or may not choose to hand out your cell phone number to clients, but a cell phone comes in handy for checking your office voice mail when you are on the road. This allows you to respond to phone messages in a prompt and professional manner.

Fax

While you need to have fax capabilities, there are a couple of different ways you can get the fax services you need. First, you can go the traditional route of buying a fax machine and installing a dedicated line in your office for the fax machine. This, of course, requires the cost of purchasing and maintaining the fax machine. An alternative route is to invest in an e-fax service where you can send and receive faxes online. There are several e-fax services that provide you with a dedicated phone number for your faxes, such as eFax (**www.efax.com**), MyFax (**www.myfax.com**), and RingCentral (**www.ringcentral.com**). Instead of having to install a second phone line in your office, the e-fax service accepts the faxes for you and sends them to your e-mail. Opening your e-faxes is as easy as opening an e-mail, and you have the option of reading the fax online or printing it. E-fax services also allow you to send faxes online. If it is a hard-copy document that you need to send, then you will need a scanner to scan the document into your computer. If you are faxing a word processing document or document already on your computer, then you can send it directly from your computer via fax. These services start at $20 a month and go up from there depending on if there is a monthly limitation on the faxes you can send and receive.

Printer, copier, fax, and scanner

All-in-one printer, copier, scanner, and fax machines may be a viable option for your office. When you have high-volume printing projects where hundreds of copies need to be made, you can also use an office store such as FedEx Office or Office Depot to help you with the project. Your other option is to buy separate machines for your printing, copying, faxing, and scanning needs. The good part of an all-in-one machine is that for a couple hundred dollars or less you will have all of the equipment you need. The downside is if one of the parts breaks then you either have to replace or repair the broken role of the machine or buy a replacement machine.

Computer and computer software

Your computer may be the heartbeat of your consulting business. You will need to use your computer for almost all aspects of your business from conducting Internet research to creating client correspondence such as letters, proposals, reports, presentations, and more. If you have to buy a new computer, make sure that you invest in the best computer possible and that it has software capabilities such as word processing, spreadsheets, database management, and some graphic capabilities for creating presentations. If you are planning on being relatively stationary then you can invest in a desktop computer. If your type of consulting work takes you out on the road on a frequent basis then you may want to consider using a laptop computer.

You can purchase software such as Microsoft® Office, or you can investigate online (and free) options such as Google Docs (**http:// docs.google.com**) where you can create and access documents online. Online offerings such as Google Docs also allow you to share and collaborate on documents with other parties. This can be a convenient option if your client or colleague is located in one area and you are located in another. It also alleviates the back and forth of having to send e-mail or faxes for each party to review, revise, and return in order to bring the project to completion. Even if your business turns you into a road warrior, other programs such as Box (**www.box.net**) allow you to access your documents from any computer. As an added convenience, when you work on a document on one computer, it automatically backs up the update so you always have access to the most recent version of the document you are working on.

Internet access

Most consultants work in one area of the country and have clients spread out throughout the United States and even across the globe. This means that Internet access is an essential part of doing business. You will need the Internet to access your business e-mail, conduct research, and keep up with what your competition is doing.

Office furniture

Take inventory of some of the furniture you may already own that you can use in your home-based or off-site office. At a very minimum, you need a spacious desk and comfortable chair. You may also wish to have a bookshelf or storage area for client files and support materials and a table to spread out work projects. Most consultants find a need for a filing cabinet as well. Other consultants find having a paperless office, where all of the documents are kept electronically, works better for them and helps to declutter their office space simultaneously. You can use Dropbox (**www.dropbox.com**), Box, and Google Docs to store and access your files electronically no matter what computer you are on. These types of programs also have document collaboration and sharing features, so you can give clients access to certain documents.

Business supplies

The other basic business supplies you need may seem like obvious choices but are items that should not be overlooked as you set up your office.

- **Writing instruments:** Make sure you have a supply of your favorite pens and pencils on hand for everything from taking notes while on the phone with a client to signing client contracts. If you use a whiteboard or chalkboard as part of your brainstorming sessions then you also want to have a supply of colored markers, chalk, and an eraser readily available to you in your office.

- **Paper:** First, standard copier paper is a must for a consultant office. You may wish to buy your paper by the case or at a minimum by the ream. The last thing you want to do is run out of paper in the middle of a huge client project with a deadline looming. Second, you may want to have some fancier 24-pound paper on hand for creating letters to clients. Depending on your style, you may also want to have spiral-bound notebooks or pads of paper available.

- **Paper fasteners:** A stapler, staples, paper clips (large and small), binder clips, rubber bands, and tape are all essentials to a consulting office. Preparing written reports for clients in duplicate or stapling two-page contracts together are two of the reasons you need some fastening devices available to you in your office.

- **Envelopes:** Generally, standard size #10 mailing envelopes are sufficient for mailing out everything from client invoices to contracts. If you find yourself mailing larger items, you may want to invest in 10- by 13-inch or 9- by 12-inch mailing envelopes. If you plan on running the envelopes through your printer, make sure the envelopes are compatible with your printer.

- **File folders:** If you plan on maintaining your files and records in a filing cabinet then you need hanging folders and file folders. Hanging and file folders come in various sizes and colors so you can try out different options to find the right ones for you or use a color coding system for your filing needs.

Professional Help and Support

Once you have your office space chosen and stocked with the necessary equipment and supplies, it is time to build a network of professionals to help support and run your business. The extent of the support system you need to build depends on whether you are planning on being a solo entrepreneur in a home-based business or if you are establishing a formal office setting. For example, if you plan on leasing an office space, you may need to hire an assistant to man the phone and deal with walk-in traffic (deliveries, mail, maintenance, and cleaning) while you are out of the office. No matter what type of office space you choose as the right option for your business, there are certain professionals you need to have on your team.

The three main business essentials for professional support are an accountant, lawyer, and banker. Finding the best one available for your business can be a challenge, but it can also be the bridge that connects the gap between your business and its success. These types of professionals usually have a broad range of experience working with various types of business owners, which can be beneficial to your company because they can provide advice. These types of professionals can also be a good source of referral business for you because they do interact with various types of people and businesses on a daily basis. When you set out on your search for an attorney, accountant, and banker for your business needs, there are some items to keep in mind:

- **Experience and qualifications:** Try to avoid hiring someone who simply dabbles in law, accounting, or banking as hobby; focus on hiring professionals who are dedicated to the industry. Make sure they have experience working with other consultants as well as other types of businesses before agreeing to work with them.

- **Availability:** Having access to the professional when you need them is another important consideration. If you hire someone who has so many clients he or she never has time for you, then you may as well not have hired someone to begin with.

- **Cost:** Expect to pay more for professionals with more skill and experience than the competition, but you should be able to shop and compare until you find a professional with the right combination of skill, experience, and afford-able pricing.

- **Integrity:** You also want to establish relationships with professionals that possess the same moral and ethical standards you have. You want to establish and run your business with integrity and ethics so surround yourself with professionals that can help you accomplish this.

- **Compatibility:** Because you have to work directly with these professionals for your business needs, you also need to make sure that you are compatible. You should feel comfortable talking with the professional and that you get along with them when you need advice or work with them on resolving a business issue.

Always ask for references and do your due diligence before hiring an accountant, lawyer, or banker for your business needs. When you ask for references, be sure that the references are similar to your business (home-based or consultants). Ask for at least three references from each professional who fits your criteria. Always, always, always check the references that the professionals provide to you. Inquire as to what business the reference is in, how long they have been working with the professional, and how the professional has positively contributed to their business.

Accountant

The majority of consultants starting and running a business are not experts in accounting. If this is you then it is imperative that you hire an accountant to help you start and maintain the financial records for your business. Even if math is your forte, you should consider hiring a professional accountant to keep your books for you. Delegating this important duty to a professional allows you to focus on revenue-generating business activities rather than worrying about paying your state sales tax, filing 1099 reports, or generating a profit and loss statement for your business.

One of the primary downfalls that small businesses encounter is maintaining inaccurate and inefficient business and financial records. Having a professional accountant on your team can help to ensure the success of your business. Accurate records help to keep you on the path to success and the advice that an accountant offers you helps guide you in the right direction. An accountant in a consulting business typically performs five main tasks:

1. **Small business startup accounting, sale of a business, or the purchase of a business:** An accountant can establish your business books and record-keeping system so you start out on the right foot. When and if you sell your business, the accountant can help to show the potential buyer

and the buyer's accountant how financially sound the business is, where the profits for the business come from, and the assets and liabilities the business has. Finally, if you are purchasing an existing consulting business, the accountant can review the financial records of the business to tell you if the purchase is a wise investment.

2. **Create and implement an accounting system:** A professional accountant can assess the needs of your business to create and implement an accounting system that best fits your business needs.

3. **Prepares, reviews, and audits the financial statements of the business:** Professional accountants have the know-how to accurately prepare your financial records to make sure you are compliant with the IRS and state tax regulations. The accountant can also review and audit the company financial records to offer you advice on changes you need to make in your business and to ensure you are compliant with the laws in case you are ever audited.

4. **Tax planning and appeals:** There are many tax laws and loopholes that accountants are knowledgeable about, and they use these to help you appropriately plan to minimize your tax obligations. If you run into a tax issue, the accountant also helps you appeal any tax issues that may arise.

5. **Prepares income tax returns:** Businesses, depending on how the legal structure of the business (sole proprietorship, corporation, LLC), have to file tax forms throughout

the year, including the annual federal business tax returns. The accountant prepares and files these forms on your behalf and makes sure you meet the deadlines for each tax form filing.

One of the best ways to find an accountant for your consulting business is to ask family members and friends, especially those who have a small business. You want to interview accountants as you would any professional you are adding to your business support team and make sure you shop around and compare several different accountants before deciding on which one is right for you.

You may be wondering what the difference is between an accountant and a certified public accountant (CPA). A CPA is a professional accountant who has taken and passed a state exam covering business law, accounting, taxes, and auditing. CPAs are also required to have a college degree, although some states allow CPAs to substitute work experience for a college degree.

Is a CPA better than accountant for your consulting business? The right answer for your business depends on your business needs. Professional accountants can be as sufficient as CPAs when it comes to establishing and maintaining your business books and financial records. It is better to assess the experience of each accountant or CPA you interview and how his or her experience relates to your business needs.

Lawyer

Even if your business is starting out with one employee (you), a lawyer is an essential member of your business support team.

In fact, hiring an attorney is a task you may want to accomplish before you do anything else, including choosing the legal form of your business entity, because a lawyer can help guide you to establish your business in the most beneficial manner for your needs. The role of an attorney in your business can be as small or large as you choose it to be. Most people think of an attorney when they need court representation, but there are several additional tasks attorneys can perform, with some keeping you out of going to court. Attorney tasks include:

- Helping you choose the right business entity
- Creating and reviewing business contracts
- Working on issues that may and do arise with your employees
- Assisting with business credit issues including bankruptcy
- Addressing client complaints and issues

Banker

With money playing a pivotal role in your consulting business, it is no wonder that hiring a banking institution that fits your needs is imperative. Your business bank handles your checking and savings accounts for your business, but the role of the bank goes beyond these basic business needs. The bank also acts as the tax depository service for your business tax payments and may be a lender to your business if it needs funds to start, grow, or for another need. Generally, you want to establish a relationship with a bank that has a local presence so you have easy access to them when you need them. Financial institutions range from banks and credit unions to credit card, commercial finance, and consumer finance companies.

Banking institutions: Banks, savings and loans, and even commercial banks are traditional financial institutions that most businesses turn to when establishing various types of financial accounts. As a small consulting company, you may wish to turn to the bank where you keep your personal accounts. Because you already have an established relationship with the institution, it can make it easier and more convenient to handle your business transactions there as well. Check with your personal banking institution first to see what type of small business products and services it offers.

Credit unions: Credit unions operate on a similar level to banks; the only difference is the members of the credit union own it. Credit unions tend to offer the same products and services as a traditional bank but at a reduced rate. The issue you may run up against with a credit union is that oftentimes they offer personal accounts and services but may not offer the same extent of business products or services, and therefore may not fit your business financial needs.

Commercial finance company: Commercial finance companies deal with the leasing or financing of major equipment. Depending on the type of consultant you are, you may or may not need to establish a relationship with this type of finance company. When it comes to leasing, these types of finance companies can provide significant tax advantages, so it is something you need to be aware of in case a need arises.

Credit card companies: In most cases, small business owners are personally responsible for credit card debt and loans for the business. Many consultants use business credit cards and business credit card loans to finance the startup costs of their business. The disadvantage to using this type of credit is that the interest rates are typically much higher than standard bank, credit union, and other business loans.

Consumer finance companies: Consumer finance companies lend to those who have bad credit, have defaulted on previous loans, or have a hard time obtaining a loan from more traditional lending institutions. Because these types of borrowers are higher risk for the finance company, consumer finance companies tend to charge higher interest rates than other types of lending institutions, and the terms of the loan tend to be shorter and less attractive. Generally, a consumer finance company should be the last stop on your list and only if you cannot obtain credit or loans from one of the other types of institutions.

☐ **Checklist**
☐ Decide which type of office setup is the most beneficial to your business needs.
☐ Make a list of the furniture, equipment, and supplies you already have for your office and the items you need to purchase.
☐ Gather information on and interview members of your support team including attorneys, bookkeepers or accountants, and bankers.
☐ Choose the right professional for your business in each category.

Chapter 4

Putting Your Business Plan in Writing

In this chapter, you will:

- Learn each component that makes up a professional business plan.

- Create a custom business plan for your consulting business that you can use as a guide for running your business and as a tool to obtain business loans and attract investors.

- Get a glimpse of the marketing plan portion of the business plan.

- Discover ways to implement, stick to, and modify your plan.

"If you fail to plan, you plan to fail." As a consultant, planning should be in your blood, and this innate sense should relate to planning the launch of your consulting business as well. While you may be anxious to get your consulting business up and running, creating a written business plan is an essential task you need to complete before you open your business. The business plan helps you create a guide that thoroughly describes your consulting business now and where you want to guide the business in the future. You would not plan a long road trip without first plotting out the most direct route from Point A to Point B. The same holds true for leading a consulting business to success: You need to plot out how you are going to take your business from Point A (where it is now) to Point B (where you want it to be).

Benefits of a Business Plan

The benefits of giving a written business plan for your business far outweigh the time investment of putting the plan together. One of the primary benefits to writing a business plan for your consulting business is that it provides you with a clear definition of your business ideas and the direction of your business. A business vision is a way to keep your business clear in your own mind, to share with current or future employees of your business, and to help you obtain financing for your business. A business plan establishes a solid foundation for you to build on your consulting business and helps you plan how to deal with problems, obstacles, and issues that may arise. A written business plan also lays out a realistic view of what your purpose is and how to overcome potential obstacles in getting it started and maintaining it by illustrating the time investment required to create a successful consulting business. Other advantages of putting together a business are it brings all of the financial data for starting and running the business together because it forces you to analyze the costs to start and maintain the business, as well as perform an analysis of staffing needs now and as you grow, including what types of staff positions you need to fill or outsource and how you will hire and train the staff in order for them to make a significant impact on your business.

While writing a business plan is not a difficult task, there is a lot of thought and research that needs to happen before you write the first word. Gathering this information up front helps you write a more effective and higher quality business plan. Before you jump right in to creating the business plan for your consulting company, write down the answers to these five questions. Answering these questions will set you in the right direction for writing your plan.

1. Is there a local, regional, or industry need for the type of consulting you wish to provide? Is there a niche your business will be able to serve? Does the consulting service you plan to put together fill this need?

2. Is there an adequate market for your consulting business to turn a sufficient profit? Is there too much competition or will it be too expensive to advertise to attract enough customers? Will your customers be able to pay for the services you are offering?

3. Will you be readily available to service your customers? If your consulting business will have a specific location, will it be centrally located to benefit your customers? Is the location affordable?

4. Do you have the skills and resources available to serve your customers? What materials and products do you require to serve your customers' needs?

5. What differentiates your consulting business from your competition? What is your USP? What does your business offer a client that is better or different from your competition? Do you have enough qualified employees to provide the service?

You may need to take some time to research adequately the answers to these questions, but knowing the answers places you in a good position to start working on your business plan. Consider the facts you uncover during your research when writing your business plan. Not only does this paint a realistic view of the viability of starting your consulting business, but it also puts the facts and figures into a comprehensive document you can take to a lender to obtain financing for your consultant business.

CASE STUDY: HOW A BUSINESS PLAN CAN HELP

Cathy Iconis, CPA
Tucker, GA 30084
404-496-8944
www.cathyiconis.com

Cathy Iconis offers Virtual CFO and accounting consulting services to help small businesses analyze their financial status in order to make better business operating decisions. Virtual CFO and accounting services operate the accounting functions for business clients from their own office. She also assists accounting departments and CPA firms with overflow work they have on different projects.

Iconis was working in the finance department of a global construction company before venturing out on her own. Once she got pregnant, she tried to work out a flexible schedule including working from home, but the company was unable to provide that for her. Iconis always wanted to work with small businesses, so she took advantage of the situation and decided to stay home with her daughter and start her own business.

When Iconis started her business, she did not write or have a business plan written for her. The lack of a business plan has affected her business because she feels that the business has not grown as quickly because she did not formalize a plan.

"I feel like I'm gradually creating a plan — by figuring out what works and what doesn't from experience," Iconis said. "I tell myself that I didn't write a plan because I wouldn't have known most of the answers until I started doing it. Honestly, that is probably a cop-out, but that is the path I have taken. I probably would have been better prepared for different situations if I had taken the time to prepare a plan."

One of the items a business plan would have helped Iconis address is the way she charges clients. She first established an hourly rate for clients, which still works great for overflow work for accounting firms and accounting departments. This fee structure has not been as successful with Virtual CFO and controller clients, however. With these clients, she is now shifting to a set number of hours that she dedicates to each client each month, for which she charges a flat monthly rate.

After gaining experience working with small business owners, Iconis realized that these businesses are going in many different directions, and she believes that a set monthly fee makes it more likely they will utilize her services. She knows that if clients agree to the monthly fee, then they are serious about working with her. Her clients also pre-pay the monthly fee, so if they do not use the time in that month, then they lose it. Iconis feels this helps to keep clients motivated to get her the information and feedback that she needs in order to help them.

Overall Components of a Business Plan

A business plan is made up of several different parts. At the end of the business plan, all of these parts work in conjunction with one another to create a written guide you can use to start and run your business.

1. **Company description:** One of the first components of the business plan is a complete description of your company and the services it offers to your clients.

2. **Marketing plan:** One of the main focus points of the business plan is the marketing plan contained within the business plan. The marketing portion of the business plan is an outline of marketing efforts to advertise your consulting business to attract the customers you are seeking.

3. **Business structure:** This portion of the business plan provides a detailed explanation of how you plan to structure and manage your business.

4. **Financials:** The final component of the business plan is a detailed explanation and outline of the expected startup and operational costs for your consulting business. This portion of the plan describes how you will manage the expenses and costs of your business.

While this is an overview of the contents of the business plan, there are a lot of subcategories and information that falls into each of these four categories. The rest of this chapter walks you through the outline of a business plan and guides you on what specific and detailed information each portion of the outline should contain.

A business plan is always a work in progress. While you need a starting point for your business plan to obtain necessary financing and to launch your consulting business, it is typical and advisable to adjust your business plan throughout the first year of business. Because the business plan contains both short- and long-term goals for your business, your goals may change when you need to refocus your short-term efforts. The short-term efforts may also have an effect on your long-term goals.

Update the plan by replacing old ideas that did not work with new ideas. Adjustments to the plan should reflect lessons learned from your first few months in business and in an effort to serve your customers better.

A basic outline for a business plan includes:

- Cover page
- Table of contents
- Business description
- Market analysis
- Competitive analysis
- Marketing plan
- Management plan
- Operating procedures
- Personnel
- Business insurance
- Financial data
- Loan applications
- Capital, equipment, and supply list
- Balance sheet
- Break-even analysis
- Pro forma income projections (profit and loss statements)
- Three-year summary
- Detail by month for the first year in business
- Detail by quarters for the second and third years in business

- Assumptions used to make projections
- Pro forma cash flow statements
- Supporting documents
- Tax returns of principals for the last three years
- Personal financial statement
- In the case of a franchised business, a copy of the franchise contract and all supporting documents provided by the franchisor
- Copy of proposed lease or purchase agreement for building space
- Copy of licenses and other legal documents
- Copy of résumés of all principals
- Copies of letters of intent from suppliers and vendors

The companion CD-ROM (and the Appendix) has a copy of a consulting business plan, so you can modify it to create your own custom plan.

Cover page

Think of the cover page of your business plan like the cover of a book or your chance to make a good first impression. In essence, the cover page sets the tone and expectations for what the reader can expect the document to contain. A cover should include the title of the business plan and include the name and logo for your business. Also include the date the document is created, your name as the owner of the company, the business address, telephone number, e-mail address, and website.

Table of contents

Following your cover page, include a table of contents to present the contents of the business plan in an organized and logical manner. It shows the reader that you are serious and organized in your thought process for creating and running your consulting business. A table of contents also makes it easy for the reader to find and access information they are looking for in the business plan. A sample table of contents includes:

- Business description
- Market analysis
- Competitive analysis
- Marketing plan
- Management plan
- Financial plan
- Appendices
  - Financial statements (list out each statement contained in the plan)
  - Supporting documents (list out each document contained in the plan)

Business description

Many consultants and other types of business owners find it difficult to describe their business when putting together the business plan. This really does not have to be an overwhelming process. In fact, the description of your business may be as little as one paragraph or may stretch as much as one page. The main question you need to answer when describing your business is: What type of consulting business do you plan on having? When answering this question, some of the details you want to include are:

- The legal structure of the business

- The company mission and vision, which describes the purpose for your business to exist

- Specific and measurable goals for the business

- An overview of the business product and service offerings

- Whether the business is new, a franchise, or you are taking over an existing company

- The name of the business and the owner(s)

Market analysis

The market analysis section of the business plan addresses the industry or companies you will be catering to with your consulting services. This area of the business plan probably requires the most amount of research because it requires you to gather data on the consulting specialty or industry you have chosen for your business focus. Trade journals that cater to consulting, *Consulting* magazine (**www.consultingmag.com**), and trade journals for the industry you plan on serving are all helpful resources for gathering this type of information. Consulting research firms, such as Kennedy Information (**www.kennedyinformation.com**), compile data and research to help you analyze what is happening in your industry as well. The market analysis contains:

- The industry or niche you are targeting
- The current state of the industry or niche (stable, growing, or declining)
- The industry's future that may affect the success of your business
- The demographics of your current and potential customers
- How big your potential market is

- The dollar value of the piece of the market that is potential business for you

Competitive analysis

The next area of the business plan is a review and analysis of your competition. You can learn a lot about the direction of your business based on what your competition is (and is not) doing. You first need to identify who your competitors are, then you need to conduct an in-depth analysis of their business operations. Determine the answers to these questions to help in your analysis:

- What areas, either geographically, industry, or niche, do your competition serve?

- How does your consulting business differ from your competition?

- How does the competition price their products and services and how does this compare to your pricing?

- What experience do your competitors have and how does this compare to your experience?

- Do the competitors have strong name recognition among the target market audience, and how much market share does each competitor have of the market?

- What stage is the competitor in (growing, declining, or stable)?

- Why would a customer choose you over your competition? What is your USP?

- What is your competition doing to market its products and services? What is and is not working?

- What are the strengths and weaknesses of your competition and what are your own?

Marketing plan

The marketing plan portion of the business plan provides an in-depth look on all of the advertising and public relations efforts you will use to make potential clients aware of your business. You may offer the best consulting service in the country or the world, but if nobody knows you exist then you are going to have a hard time making sales and making money. Because the marketing plan plays such a pivotal role in your business plan, Chapter 10 is devoted to developing and implementing a strategic marketing plan to promote your consulting business. To give you a basic overview of the marketing section of the business plan, this section of the plan contains:

- A description of your target audience(s)

- The menu of products and services you offer along with the pricing

- The types of the marketing and advertising efforts you will use to build your brand, garner the attention of your target market, and convert them into customers

Management plan

The management plan details how you will structure and operate your business. One of the best ways to list these details is by envisioning what running your own consulting business looks like. Do you see yourself working alone handling every facet of the business? Do you want or need to hire employees to handle various tasks, or can you outsource certain tasks to freelancers and third parties without hiring employees?

While many factors go into creating your management plan, the first thing you need to consider is that *you* have to be a good manager in order to make your consulting business successful. Some of the basic characteristics you need to possess (or learn to possess) are commitment, dedication, persistence, and good decision-making skills. When you are running your own consulting business, some decisions have to be made instantly without time to carefully weigh all of the pros and cons. On top of managing yourself, it is also imperative that you can handle the business finances and manage others. Possessing, acquiring, and refining all of these skills requires hard work and patience. The management portion of your business plan is ultimately the foundation you are building for the way your business is run.

When you are putting together this portion of the plan, now is the time to be honest with yourself. It is imperative that you analyze whether you have the skills necessary to manage your business. If you are lacking some skills or some need to be polished, this is the time to own up to it and figure out how to make your skills better — take a class, read a book, or work with a business coach.

For the most part, novice consultants may not have experience running a business if they have always been employees. After assessing your own skills, you can quickly see what type of employees you may need to hire in order to round out and complement your own skills. This should create a well-rounded team that works well together and can handle the extensive responsibilities of running your consulting business.

When writing your management plan, take the time to answer these questions:

- Do you have the background and the experience to run a successful consulting business?
- What are your shortcomings in running a business, and how will you compensate for those shortcomings?
- Which employees, if any, will you need to add to your management team?
- How will your employees' strengths and weaknesses complement your shortcomings?
- What tasks will you assign to each member of the team?
- How will you outline your employees' responsibilities?
- What amount of help do you need to get your business started?
- How will you hire and train employees to be part of your team?
- What salary and benefits will you provide to each team member?

By answering these questions, you can determine how you intend to run your consulting business. Your answers will serve as a guide for you to reach your business goals. Creating this part of the plan can also act as a handbook for employees you may hire in the future.

If you are starting a franchise consulting company, some additional questions you need to answer include:

- Does the management package address your questions and concerns?

- How will the corporate office help you develop your management team?

- What type and amount of assistance does corporate provide on an ongoing basis?

When considering a franchise, be sure to include any specifics from their business plan into your own business plan because many franchises have requirements you need to follow. Some franchise requirements include how many employees you need to hire, which roles the employees need to fill, the training requirements for you as the owner, the training requirements for each employee, and ongoing education and training required. Because a franchise has existing plans in place, including details from the franchise's business plan can also help you start your business off in the right direction.

Financial data

The starting point for your business financial plan is to create a realistic budget for your business. Because a financial plan includes your startup and operating costs, you need to determine how much money you need to open your consulting company for business and how much it is going to cost you to keep the business open week after week, month after month, and year after year.

Startup budget

When you first start your consulting business, you will have one-time, startup costs for your business to get it up and running. For example, you may need to purchase equipment to get the business started, but once you buy the equipment, you will not have the expense again until you need to replace it. Keep the answers to these questions in mind when figuring out the startup costs of your business:

- How much money do you have available?

- How much will it cost to start a franchise (and should you be planning to do so)?

- What other fees or purchases do you have to make to open your doors for business?

- How much money do you need to stay open for business for the next six months to a year?

If you are buying into a consulting franchise, you also need to ask yourself:

- Does the corporation have requirements for your operating and startup costs?

- Does the corporation set your sales and profit goals for you?

- What sales and profit margin are you expected to reach and maintain to hold onto your business franchise?

Each portion of the financial management plan needs a thorough explanation of your projections and how you came to the figures included in the plan. You may need to talk to a financial adviser or an accountant to help you calculate accurate facts and figures. These professionals also provide you with advice, review your research, and formulate reports about your organization to help refine your plan. Be sure to have your preliminary costs, facts, and figures together before seeking the advice of a financial adviser or accountant so they can review the numbers with you and make sure that they are realistic. It also helps the professionals to provide you with the right advice and guidance to achieve your goals.

Operating budget

If you are running your consulting business out of your home office, your operating budget and expenses are probably going to be much lower than if you are renting office space. Take a look at the amount of money you have available to start and run your business, including any furniture and equipment you need to purchase and how much it costs you to keep your phone, lights, and Internet service on. Once you put these figures together, you will have a good handle on the amount of an operating budget required to keep your business afloat.

You should also have a cushion built into your budget in case unexpected expenses arise. The additional cushion of funds can help you keep your financial plan on more sound ground, which can ultimately keep your business from faltering or failing. As you are building your operating budget, revisit the amount of money you have on hand to see if you have enough money to cover the operating business expenses for six months to a year. If not, you may need to take out a loan or find a way to raise the amount you have in savings.

Your financial plan should include:

- Information on pending loan applications
- The value of your equipment and supplies
- An up-to-date balance sheet
- A break-even analysis
- A detailed profit-and-loss statement (P&L)

The financial portion of your business plan also needs to include an income statement and cash flow projections for the first three years of your business, including back-up documentation and data. You will want to break the statement out on a month-by-month basis, by the quarter, and annually. Compiling these figures can be challenging, but the benefit of building and maintaining a financially sound business far outweighs the time it takes to prepare the statements. Showing that you have a detailed plan for your business also helps you prove to potential lenders and other investors that your business has a solid foundation and is a good investment for them to make a loan on. With the many variables involved in generating the estimates and projected figures for your business, there is not a set formula for coming up with the numbers. One way to get an idea of projected figures is to look at sample consulting company business plans that cover the same industry. One online resource for sample business plans is Bplans.com (**www.bplans.com**). Again, your fee schedules and service offering would have to be identical in order to project the same figures as the sample, but you can use the sample as a guide.

Realism is an important factor when you are compiling the financial data for the company. These estimates also do not tend to be carved in stone, so you may need to adjust this information as you open for business and compare actual costs with the estimates you have projected. Be conservative and realistic when compiling your revenue figures. While high expected income numbers may initially impress potential lenders into investing in your business, if your business is not able to generate a big enough profit, you will have a hard time covering all of your business expenses, including paying back your loan.

☐ Checklist

☐ Write, edit, and consistently update your business plan as your business continues to expand.

Chapter 5

Setting Your Fees

In this chapter, you will:

- Learn the different ways you can charge clients and how much to charge for your services.

- Uncover how to price your services by doing competitive research of the industry or location.

- How to establish a fee agreement with your clients, how to collect fees, and how to collection the remaining fees.

Before you open your consulting business, you need to determine what services you plan on offering your clients and how you are going to charge for them. For most consultants, setting fees is one of the most difficult tasks in getting started. You may be able to tackle a company's low profit and high loss situation and help them figure out ways to make their business more profitable, but when it comes to setting your fees, you may be at a loss on where to start. The good news is that there is not a right and wrong answer to what you should or can charge for your services. You do have to find the balance, though, between what your time is worth and what your clients are willing to pay for the services you provide. While at first this may sound like an easy task, if you set your prices too low, the end result may be a surplus of low-paying work that takes a lot of your time and barely turns a profit. On the other hand, if you set your costs too high, you may not get enough business to turn a profit.

Competitive Research

One of the best places to start with setting your consulting fees is to do some competitive research. Also, take the time to read about each consultant's experience and background to see how it compares to your own experience and background. The more experience you have to offer your clients, the higher fee you may be able to warrant for your services. As you start your research, you will also find that different consultants charge differently — by the hour, by the project, or by the service. While you may not be able find enough consultants who offer the same industry or niche services you plan on offering, you can get an idea of how much consultants in general charge.

Most consulting companies do not list their fee schedules online, while others list at least a range of fees that provide an idea of what they charge. For those that do not list their fees online, you may want to make some phone calls or send an e-mail to speak directly with the consultants. Explain that you are starting a consulting business and are seeking advice on how they price their services. You will find that most consultants are more than willing to share information with you. Find out not only how they charge clients, but also their reasons for doing so. For example, a consultant may say they charge by the project because clients are leery of getting charged by the hour because they feel they may get taken advantage. Keep in mind that every consultant is different. You can use the information you obtain from your competitive research to form an educated opinion and base your decision on setting your own fees. Later in this chapter, you will learn more about the fee schedules consultants use to get a better idea of how you can set your fees.

After you decide how you are going to charge clients and how much you will charge for your services, you also need to do the following:

Establish and maintain an accurate fee schedule: The fees you set must allow you to meet the financial goals of your consultant business. Not only do the fees need to cover your business financial needs, but the fees also need to cover your personal financial needs as well. Add up all of your business and personal expenses to first determine how much money the business needs to bring in to break even. Then you can work backward to determine how many clients you need and how much you need to charge.

Embrace and believe in your rates: The first step to being able to sell your clients on the value of your services and to pay the fees you have set is to believe in the value of your experience and service. Once you convince yourself that you are the best person to handle their problems, you will excel in your business and be able to convince clients the value of what you offer is more important than the actual numbers.

Accept that you are worthy: Accept the fact that you are worth the investment clients are making in you. Stop worrying and being afraid about the rates you have set and about communicating the rates to your clients. Your experience, time, and skills are valuable resources to your clients, and it is up to you to convert prospects into paying clients.

If you are still struggling with setting your rates, you are not alone in the struggle. This is one of the most difficult parts of becoming a consultant. Once you set your rates, stick to the fee schedule you have set so you are able to meet your business and personal financial goals. For example, assume your goal is to generate $75,000 each year. Here is a break down of a financial plan:

Yearly: $75,000
Weekly: $1,442.31 ($75,000 / 52 weeks)
Daily: $288.46 ($1,442.31 / 5 days)

If you charge $50 per hour for your services, this means you have to be able to charge a client for almost six hours of work each day.

$$\frac{\$288.46}{\$50} = 5.77 \text{ hours}$$

Once you see the figures in writing, it may lead you through multiple revisions to determine a set price. You will need to refine these goals as your business progresses and your experience widens. Other reasons you may change your fees or fee schedule is if you add additional services or products to your menu or reduce the work you provide to clients. Changing your rates is not a daily or even monthly practice, but you should review your pricing once or twice a year, especially as you become more established in your business and industry.

You will also need to think about how this pricing positions you the marketplace in contrast to your competition. In most markets, you will not be the only consultant available to hire for the project the client has at hand, so you will need to price accordingly to what your competition is charging. Look at it from the point of view of a client. When clients are comparing consultants and all of the candidates are equal, the client is likely to select the least expensive service available — it is common sense. If you have the same references and offer the same services as your competition, chances are good that the client will select the consultant who can offer the lowest price.

You need to provide a reason for a client to select you over the other consultants available because clients tend to focus on the less-expensive price rather than weighing the pros and cons between consultants. Because a cheaper price can lead to lower quality service, it is important that you can convince the client that your more expensive price comes with a superior level of service. You have to offer something unique, something the client wants but perhaps has not vocalized or considered. If you provide a customized solution to the client, he or she will likely value your service offering over the competition. If you cannot find a differentiation strategy to work with then you may need to consider adjusting your price level to be more competitive.

It may take time for you to refine the skills required to assess and analyze your competition. For example, you and several other consultants submit proposals for the same client project and you find out the client chose a consultant you consider as an equal, even though the other consultant's proposal was higher. Chances are good that the consultant delivered a customized solution to the client, therefore landing the job. You may also run into a problem if you are offering the same services and charging the same fees as your competition. In these circumstances, other consultants can only stay competitive with you (and you with them) if you offer less-expensive proposals, which means you are constantly undercutting your price in order to win the client over. Over time, this can have an adverse effect on your business and personal finances. Here are some tips for illustrating the value of your services and fees:

1. **Add value to your proposal:** Figure out a way to differentiate your services from your competition so your proposal stands out from the rest. For example, charge the client for five objectives, but deliver six. Instead of delivering the project in the expected two months, offer delivery in six weeks — but make sure it is a realistic promise you are making. These small things can make a considerable impact on the client's view of you and help you build your reputation.

2. **Offer and provide the best customer service available:** Every client wants to feel as if he or she is important to you. Make the client feel like your No. 1 priority by wowing your client with superior customer service. Always do what you say, meet deadlines, keep in touch, and provide clients with a positive attitude from when they are prospective clients to until the project is complete.

3. **Stand out from the competition:** Find ways to be unique in what you offer and how you get the job done. Offer 24-hour availability, implement changes based on customer feedback, or do the legwork for your client. Any consultant can offer the basic services a client is looking for, but the consultant who gets called back to help again is the one who exceeds expectations.

4. **Always do your best work:** No matter what, deliver the best product possible *every time.* If you are helping a client with a project, he or she needs to be your highest priority, and the client should feel that way. This means sticking to your promises, delivering on time, and doing what you say you will do. These small things make a significant impact on the success your client sees in the work you do.

5. **Consider the long-term ramifications:** Instead of having to land a steady stream of new clients, a better solution is to rely on your current clients to offer you repeat and referral business. In fact, it costs five times more to get a new client than it is to keep an existing client. Focus on providing the highest quality work and resources you can so that you get referrals. Position yourself as available and consistent. If you do the work to the client's satisfaction (or exceed client expectations), he or she will continuously come back when they need work, keeping you busy for less money and effort than always trying to land new clients.

Client Perceptions of Your Worth

In the businesses world of consulting, you are only worth what a client is willing to pay. When you first start your business, you may not know what the magic number is, and the magic number may vary from client to client. Spending some time working out specific ways to calculate a range of figures helps you feel more comfortable in setting your fees and provides you with some flexibility when talking about your fees with clients. In order to estimate what your clients believe your services are worth, you need to find out what clients believe your service can provide. While the quality of a service may seem high on the list of necessities, some clients value dollar amounts more than they do the quality of a service. The only way you will be able to find out the perceptions your clients have about your service is to talk with them.

First, find out about the specific needs of the client you are talking with. Some clients may know or think they know what their needs are. Ask questions and probe the client until you figure out what their needs are. In many instance, the client has a different view of their needs and your services than you do. Having those two different perceptions (your view and their view) can complicate the process, but you can work on molding and changing your clients' perceptions to help show them how your services can resolve their problem. While you probably will not be able to read your client's mind as to what they are willing to pay for your services, you can assess what their needs are and then put a price tag on the value of the services you can provide to them. Once you determine why the client would be in a position to hire a consultant, you can help the client to understand that there are basically three ways they can fulfill their need:

1. They can assign the task to an existing employee, which adds new responsibilities to an employee who already has an existing set of responsibilities within the company.

2. They can hire an additional employee to tackle the issue. This equates to paying an additional salary and possibly employee benefits such as health insurance and retirement plans. The company is also responsible for providing a workspace for the new employee to perform his or her job. This can add up to a significant expense to the company's bottom line.

3. They can hire you. A consultant who has the expertise to handle the situation effectively unlike anyone else in the organization can be the fastest and most cost effective way to deal with the problem at hand successfully because the company does not have to take the consultant on as a full-time employee. This kills two birds with one stone: The consultant gets the job done quickly and effectively and saves the company money in the process.

Benefits to hiring consultants include the following:

- You are an independent contractor, which mean you work on an as-needed basis to save the company money.

- The consultant works hand in hand with the client to get the job accomplished. There is no boss to look over your shoulder or tell you what to do to stay on task but there is no one else to blame when the job is not done well.

- If the client is not happy with the quality of your work then they can sever the relationship and find another service provider.

- As a third party, you bring an outside and objective view, which is something that the client and other employees do not have.

- You provide clients with a clear picture about the internal and external forces on the company.

- You devote time and attention to fixing the problem or issue the client is facing, while an employee has to spend time on normal tasks as well as tackling the problem, therefore extending the time frame of both roles.

- Once a consultant's work is done, the consultant is removed from the process, unlike an employee hired to resolve the problem. You complete the work, leave, and the client pays you once.

- Clients can pick up the phone and call you when a new need arises.

- You are available to the client when needed, but you are not sitting idle and collecting a paycheck from the client when they have no need for your services.

- Consultants save the client money on job position advertising, training, salary, benefits, taxes, and more.

- Hiring a consultant costs the client less because you come in and do the job right and quickly the first time.

When you understand the myriad of reasons a consultant benefits a company, it helps you position yourself and your services as a benefit to the company, helping clients understand your value and worth. Remember, you are a very valuable asset to the clients you serve, so you are worth the company investment.

CASE STUDY: BASING FEES ON RESULTS RATHER THAN TIME

The Callidus Group
William L. Ringle, president
Gibsonia, PA
724-444-0455
www.thecallidusgroup.com

When William (Bill) Ringle found himself frustrated while wasting time in work meetings and having to deal with office politics, he thought there must be a better way for him to move on with his career. When he found himself displaced from his corporate position, he took the opportunity to make a better career path and bought into a franchise. Eventually, he sold the franchise and transitioned into opening a highly specialized consulting practice where he helps entrepreneurs and business owners to achieve better results for themselves, their families, and their team members.

Ringle runs his consulting practice from his home office. Experiencing empty nest syndrome, Ringle enjoys running the business from his den-converted office because it allows him to keep his overhead expenses to a minimum, and he takes advantage of the tax benefits associated with having a home office.

As part of the business plan he implemented when he first started his consulting firm, he included a plan for how he currently charges clients today. Rather than charge by the hour, where clients have to watch the clock like Ringle is a CPA or lawyer, he charges the client on a fixed monthly rate. He refers to his fee structure as "value-based pricing" because the monthly rate is determined by the value that the clients receive from working with him.

Ringle chose to base his pricing on value because he feels it is more about the results the business and business owner realize rather than his time. He builds relationships with clients, and his goal is to make them a client for life through the weekly mentoring sessions he has with his clients. There are times when projects arise from his mentoring sessions that are above and beyond his original work with the client. In these situations, he opts to charge by the project.

While Ringle has not created an income stream using informational products yet, his next goal is to write and publish a book.

Show a company how you save it money

The bottom line for any company is resolving its problem or issue in the fastest and most cost-effective way possible. While a client may seem to focus on the price as the bottom line, it is essential for you to focus on the value of your services. Once you establish a solid foundation on how valuable your services can be to the client, then you talk fees and figures for getting the job done.

For example: You start your meeting with a client by stating you charge $100 per hour. The client may get so hung up on the cost that they close their mind off to the rest of your conversation. Now, you have to back pedal to try to get the client to understand the value of what they are getting for the $100 per hour. If the company is paying its employees $25 an hour, you are going to have a hard time convincing them that you are saving them money when they will be paying you $100 an hour. Instead, walk into the meeting and discuss the client's need first. This allows you to gather information, such as the fact that they pay their employees

$25 per hour. You can then explain how hiring an employee to complete the role you would fulfill is going to take the employee 40 hours per week to complete at $25 an hour. Hiring you as a consultant, on the other hand, means the task is complete in one month for a total of 40 hours at $100 per hour, which is a significant cost savings for the client even though your hourly fee is four times as much.

In order to help client understand your worth, you can break it down into figures. Because money tends to talk and be the determining factor, showing a client how you save them money can be a compelling exercise in gaining their business. So, the hourly rate pay for the employee is $25 an hour, but that comes with the 35 percent (on average) the company has to pay for the fringe benefits such as health and life insurance and retirement plans. An employee also comes with the added overhead (50 percent on average) to paying for expenses such as workspace and electricity. With these additional costs, the client ends up paying about $46 an hour for an employee to tackle the issue you would be tackling as a freelance consultant.

Benefit cost per hour: $25 x .35 = $8.75
Overhead cost per hour: $25 x .50 = $12.50
Total cost per hour: $8.75 + $12.50 + $25 = $46.25

That employee is going to stay on the payroll even when the issue is resolved, while you get the job done in a total of 40 hours and in a one-month period. In effect, hiring an employee would cost the company more than $96,000 a year.

Weekly cost: $46.25 x 40 hours/week = $1,850
Yearly cost: $1,850 x 52 weeks = $96,200

Instead, if the company hires you to work 40 hours a month for $100 an hour, the company is paying $48,000 a year. This is more than a 50 percent savings to the client.

Monthly wage: $100 x 40 hours = $4,000
Yearly cost: $4,000 x 12 months = $48,000

Fee Options

With three basic ways you can charge clients for your consulting services, it is important to understand how each option works. Then you need to understand the pros and cons of each fee structure. Finally, it is vital to understand in which situations each fee structure may be most appropriate for the client and most beneficial to you and your business.

Hourly

One of the primary ways consultants charge for their services is at an hourly rate. As is the case with any fee method, there are pros and cons to using an hourly rate to charge your consulting clients. The biggest disadvantage is that clients may feel like you are taking longer to complete a project in order to inflate your fees. You may also find yourself consciously or unconsciously working more hours in order to make enough money to cover your expenses. Either way, this type of fee schedule tends to pit the consultant and the client against each other and can cause a variety of rifts.

However, you will find other clients who prefer to work on an hourly basis. This is especially the case when you correctly price your hourly rate. If you price your hourly rate too low, you may have to work twice as many hours to make enough money to live on. If you price your hourly rate too high, you may not be able to attract enough business to make enough money to live either. When you are conducting your competitive research and talking with other consultants, gather the hourly rates for the consultants who charge by the hour. Most likely, the figures you obtain from other consultants run a wide range. This range provides you with a sliding scale that you can use to determine your own rates.

You also can use two other methods to calculate a range of hourly rate possibilities. One way is to build your hourly rate from the bottom up. For example, if you were working as an employee for a company, you would probably have a set number of hours to work for each pay period. If you divide the salary by the number of hours, you can quickly determine the hourly rate you are making as an employee. So, assume your weekly (gross) salary is $1,500 and you work 40 hours per week.

Hourly rate: $1,500 / 40 = $37.50

This calculation provides you with a base rate of pay you need to charge your consulting clients in order to make a comparable income that you would make as a company employee. On top of this base rate, you need to add the cost of your health insurance, retirement plan, and other expenses. Therefore, instead of needing to charge $37.50 per hour, you may need to charge an hourly fee closer to $50 an hour in order to pay yourself as a consultant and cover your own business expenses.

Another approach to calculating your hourly fee is to build the rate per hour from the top down. If you know you need to gross a certain amount of money each month, then use this as a base figure and work your way down from this figure. So, if you know you need to bring in $10,000 per month, use this figure to determine how many hours of work you need to make this happen. Then, divide the number of hours of work per month into the amount of money you want to make to determine your hourly rate.

Hourly rate: $10,000 / 160 = $62.50

No matter which method you use, the market must have the ability to support that dollar amount to make your business profitable. If you are able to convince the client that you are the right person for the job based on your value, then the client is less likely to be concerned about what your rate is (within reason, of course). Most businesses and clients assume a 20–30 percent markup on the standard going rate for a consultant in order to receive a superior level of service. If the client believes you can provide the quality of service they are looking for, then they do not tend to mind paying premium pricing for it.

If you work with a client on an hourly basis, you may also want to institute a minimum number of hours or a minimum fee for each time you work with the client. For example: You have a client that works with you on a 30-minute basis here and there. At first, you may assume you charge half your hourly rate because you are working half the time, but when you think about it logically the situation changes. You meet with this client face-to-face for only a 30-minute session, but it takes three hours out of your time. It takes you an hour to drive each way, to and from the client, plus any wait time involved in waiting for the client to be available for the meeting and then there is the 30-minute session you are there to conduct in the first place.

By instituting a minimum number of billable hours, such as a four-hour minimum, then you are protecting and valuing your time. When you respect your time, so will current and potential clients. So for a client who only wishes to book 30 minutes of your time, the hourly fee is charged at your minimum billing rate of four hours. If you charge $50 per hour, this means the minimum amount you will make for each client is $200.

By the project

The next most popular way for consultants to charge clients is by the project. When you charge on a per-project basis, you have to spend some time assessing the clients' needs so you can provide them with a flat rate charge for the services you will be performing for the clients. Typically, a project fee requires that a predetermined set of goals and terms are met before you hand in your invoice to the company and receive the flat fee for the service. This fee structure can be beneficial to you because it allows you to be paid a flat fee rather than having to haggle with your client about the number of hours needed to complete the job. As long as you effectively price your services, it typically reduces the clients' concern about how many hours you have to work to get the job done.

On a project-basis fee structure, the client does not have to worry about how many hours of work you have put into the project, as long as you meet the goals agreed upon at the beginning of the project. The drawback of this type of fee structure for you is that if you do not determine the correct number of hours to complete the project, you may find yourself working more hours than you planned. In the end, whether the project takes you 50 or 500 hours to complete, the client pays the flat rate fee.

Another benefit of this fees structure is you can estimate your income because you are setting a flat rate. You also do not have to define how many hours you need to work on the project or worry about documenting the hours of work to the client.

Retainer fee structure

Retainers are popular fee structure with professionals such as attorneys, accountants, and consultants. A retainer is a type of flat-rate fee structure where a client pays a monthly set rate and has relatively unlimited access to you and your services. The retainer fee is typically set based on a projection of the client's needs so that the client is not overpaying and the consultant is not overworked and underpaid.

For example, a marketing consultant may charge a client a retainer fee of $2,000 per month. The client can use the consultant's marketing services as often as they like for the $2,000 per month. Even if the client does not contact or use the marketing services for month, the consultant still receives the $2,000 fee. On the other hand, if the client calls the consultant every weekday for the entire month, the consultant also receives the $2,000 retainer fee.

One of the main benefits of a retainer fee structure is it allows consultants to earn money that is not directly linked to meeting a set goal or working a set amount of hours. Clients can also benefit from this fee structure because they know they can call you at any time about any of their needs because they have retained your services without limitation.

Some consultants allow clients who do not use up the retainer fee for one month to roll it over to the next month. For example, if your client contracts you with a retainer for $10,000 of services a month, you assign a time limit for this amount of services (in your client's file, but not necessarily to the client). If in January he only uses $5,000 worth of the retainer, then the additional $5,000 balance of the retainer fee is rolled over to February. If in March the client uses $12,000 worth of your services, then he or she may be required to pay you an additional $2,000 because it exceeded the $10,000 retainer fee. Some consultants allow clients to deduct this overage amount from the next month's retainer. At the end of the year, all balances return to zero and the client starts all over again, so balances are carried from year to year. The bottom line with a retainer fee is that you still have to determine how many hours you "owe" the client in order for it to be fair for both you and the client. If you expect to earn $100 per hour and your retainer fee is $5,000 per month, then is essence you intend to allocate 50 hours per month to the client.

If you assess the amount you owe the client in exchange for the retainer fee by the project, then you need to assign a set amount to each project and that is what you owe the client in order to meet their retainer fee. For example, a client pays a freelance writer $2,000 per month. The writer keeps track of the projects she completes for the client for the month. If the projects exceed or fall short of this amount then she needs to charge or deduct this amount from the retainer fee. If the writer assigns the following costs for the projects she completes for the client, then the retainer fee for the client is used up during that month:

• 5 (500–word) articles	$450
• 10 (300–500 word) blog posts	$450
• 2 press releases	$300
• 8 pages of website copy	<u>$800</u>
	$2,000

Setting your fees on a retainer basis can be beneficial because it establishes a long-term relationship with your client at a set dollar amount. It is consistent work, which is vital to operating a financially successful consulting business. While retainer fee structures have several benefits, there are also drawbacks to this type of relationship. You can allocate a certain amount of time each month to work on your client's work and then take on additional clients to fill up some of your "free" time, but what if a retainer client is additionally needy one month? You may have difficulty getting all of your work accomplished.

Once the price is right

Once you set your rate and choose the method of charging clients, you can start working toward attracting clients. Before you pull out your megaphone and announce your business is open and accepting new clientele, it is time to establish a fee agreement and plan on your process for collecting payments from clients.

A fee agreement is a written instrument used to spell out your agreement with the client. *The companion CD-ROM includes some sample fee agreements and contracts you can modify to meet your business needs.* Determine how to space out payments for your clients and include it in the agreement or contract. For example, if you work with a client on a project and provide them with a flat rate for completing the project, you may collect a 50 percent deposit initially and the remaining 50 percent when the project is complete. Other consultants spread out the payments when milestones are met.

The key to successful payment agreements and collection is to be as detailed as possible when putting together the written agreement. Make sure your agreement spells out who you are, who the client is, the scope of the project, and the specific payment terms. Require a signature from the client and make sure that you maintain an original copy of the signed agreement in case conflicts arise in the future.

You should require a deposit from all clients before you start to work on their project. This protects you from working for free for a client who does not end up paying your invoice. Collecting a deposit up front means the client has a stake in the business you are going to do with them and reduces your chances of working for nothing. Even clients who hire you on a retainer should be required to give a deposit up front. Again, the amount of this deposit is something that has to make you and the client feel comfortable. Some consultants require their clients to pay the entire retainer amount up front, which is why they allow clients to roll over unused amounts to the following month.

If Your Rate No Longer Fits

No matter what type of fee structure you decide on, there may be circumstances where you need to change the rate you are charging a client. A rate change may occur on an individual basis or there may be circumstances where you have to change your overall rates across the board. Prices may warrant a change because the cost of living increases, you have more experience, or because a client is requiring more from you than you originally agreed upon.

As a consultant, you may find it hard to increase your rate. You may fear that a rate change will cause you to lose the clients you already have or scare away the prospects you are trying to win over. On the other hand, you may need to reduce your rates for circumstances such as a change in the market for your services where you will not be able to obtain a client at your current rate. The important thing to remember is that making changes to your rates requires a careful thought process and adequate planning. For example: If you are working with a client who now requires you to travel out of town when the original contract did not require travel, then you will incur additional costs such as a hotel room, meals, and gas. This is an instance where the company should incur these additional costs, not the consultant. This means that whether you are charging the client by the hour, per-project basis, or as a retainer, you now need to adjust the cost because the scope of your work has changed.

A fee agreement will include special circumstances or stipulations where rates may change if certain circumstances occur. This is something you want to anticipate before it happens rather than after.

When to increase

The primary reason for increasing your consulting fee is that some circumstance has arisen where it is going to eat away at your profit. There are some reasons that only apply to a specific type of consulting business, but most factors apply to any type of consulting business.

Most consultants who need to increase their rate charge it to new clients rather than increase the rate for existing clients. In essence, a new client does not see the rate increase because you are simply starting them out at the higher rate. For clients you are currently under contract with, you may need to wait until your contract is up for renewal before you can incorporate your new rates and fees. However, if there are charges unaccounted for in the contract or agreement, you will need to discuss these circumstances with your clients. In some cases, the client is willing to work with you to cover these additional costs. Other clients may walk away from your relationship because of the additional fees. Here are some reasons you should consider raising your rates:

Testing the marketplace: During the first few months of your consulting career, you will probably be testing the marketplace to see if clients are willing to pay your fee and whether your fee is adequate for the time and effort you are putting in. Setting your fees accurately means determining the right fee based on what the market is willing to pay for the services you provide. If you increase your rates, evaluate how this changes the number of clients and amount of work you have. If increasing your rate causes you to lose the majority of your clients and you no longer have enough work to sustain your career and business, then you may have to reconsider.

You underpriced your services: If your profit is suffering or you are not profiting at all, then you may have to change your rate. In this circumstance, increasing your rate is a matter of necessity because your consulting business may fail completely if you are not making enough money to exceed the amount of your expenses.

Additional expenses: Often you do not realize the costs involved with working with a client until the relationship begins. For example, you may need to have a membership in their association in order to provide service to them. Perhaps travel expenses you might not have known about ahead of time occur or the project is taking more time than your time allocation. Each of these circumstances can hinder the value of your business if you do not increase your rates.

While these are some of the reasons to increase your rates, other factors may require rate increases. The key is to remember that you should only raise your rates when you have a reason to do so.

Decreasing your rate

Reducing your consulting rates should only occur if you can still turn a profit and is in the best interest of your company. While decreased rates may be necessary, never lower your rates unless you have a solid reason for doing so. Ultimately, you still need to make a profit in order to keep your business open and to earn enough income to live. Before you consider a decrease in your rate, carefully consider how the changes may affect your ability to cover your expenses and unexpected fees associated with your business. Here are some reasons why you may need to reduce the rate that you charge to your clients:

Your services are overpriced: When you first open your consulting business, a common situation is to overprice your services for your local market. If you price your services too high for the market, then you will not attract enough clients to make your business profitable. After you have exhausted all of the possibilities of attracting clients, such as adjusting your advertising, networking with new people, and reducing your expenses, the next step is to adjust your prices down to the market level.

You want to reward your long-term clients: Sometimes it is good business to offer a discount to your long-term clients. For example, if a client refers a lot of business to you, you can reward him or her by offering a discount on your services. When you want to do something like this, it is often best to make it a one-time thing rather than a standard rate decrease. For example, you may offer a discount on your services for one month of the client's contract rather than for the entire term of the agreement. This way, you still are turning a nice profit, while showing your appreciation at the same time.

You want to network with other professionals: In some situations, you should consider offering a discount on your services, when feasible, to those you are working with in your consulting business. For example, you may want to offer a discount to a company that works with your target market. When the other professional has a client that requires your services, they tend to call on you first.

You want to get your business off the ground: There is no doubt that all beginning consultants struggle to get their first few clients under their belt, so they may price their services lower to attract the first few clients. But, during this time, you are also likely to spend money on advertising and setting up your business. For this reason, be careful about setting your costs too low, or you may be shutting the business down before it gets off the ground. Once you have started to acquire business, gradually work to build your profit margin back up because experience is a helpful tool in justifying higher rates.

Some consultants offer new clients an introductory rate on their services, which is a step that can help you establish long-term contracts with clients. However, you still need to communicate your reduced introductory rate while making sure that they know what your regular rate is to illustrate the value the client is receiving for the reduced rate. For example, in the fee agreement list your normal pricing model along with the introductory rate. Point out the savings the client is receiving by working with you and advise them it is a one-time discount for the initial service offering.

When clients want a reduced rate

You will most likely run into clients who want a reduced rate no matter how low your rates already are. Price shoppers will approach you with a quote from your competitor that is lower than your own price quote. If you have done your research, you know the fair price for your services, but even more, you know the importance of turning a profit in your business. When a client wants a reduced rate and you cannot justify it, take a stand and let them know that you are not able to provide your services at a lower rate. Keep in mind that you are responsible for setting your rates, not the client.

If you do not want to lower your rates, then say no. Explain to prospective clients that your rates are based on research, expenses, and skill, and therefore the value you add to the client warrants the higher rate. Be prepared to have and share all of the reasons why your service requires the higher rate. For example, you could say: "My rates are based on 30 years of experience in the field. Your other quote is for someone just starting out in this business." This puts it back on the client to decide if quality is worth the difference in cost to them.

In other situations, it is necessary and helpful for you to consider a counter-proposal. If they are asking for a 10 percent reduction in your fees, consider offering them a 5 percent reduction instead, as long as you still turn enough of a profit for your business. Rate reductions can be beneficial for consultants starting out. Ultimately, it is all about creating a financially successful consulting business, and if you continue to undercut your rate at the expense of the business then it is not worth it.

☐ Checklist
☐ Decide how you will charge clients for your consulting services.
☐ Conduct research on competitors to find out what they offer and their fee structure.
☐ Set your prices and fees for each service you will provide.
☐ Create a written template of your client fee agreement to use as the basis for creating a contract between you and the client and collect fees due to you.

Chapter 6

The Legalities of
Starting Your Business

In this chapter, you will:

- Learn several of the legal aspects to consider when opening a consulting business.
- Become familiar with the different business structures.
- Learn the different tax structures for each type of business entity.
- Uncover how to choose and register a business name, including trademarks.
- See how to obtain a business or occupational license.
- Deal with obtaining necessary permits for your business.
- Learn how and when to obtain an employer identification number (EIN).
- Discover how to deal with state sales tax.

Starting your business off by establishing a legal entity is the first step in the life of your business. It can save you headaches, fines, and additional fees in the future, as well as help your business to be more successful and more profitable. While the right knowledge, skills, and equipment are all necessary to run a successful business, you also need to have the right legal setup for your business. Several different factors need to be considered when determining which type of business entity is the most beneficial for your consulting business. Each legal business structure has benefits and drawbacks associated with it. When you are putting your business plan together, talk with your attorney and accountant to answer any questions you may have about establishing the legal structure of your consulting business.

Sole Proprietorship

When starting a business, this is perhaps the simplest and least expensive way to establish the legal structure of your business. To establish a sole proprietorship, all you have to do is choose a business location (be it your home or a rented space), acquire any necessary equipment, and open your doors for business. The attorney fees for setting up a sole proprietorship are far less than establishing any other type of business entity, and you can typically set up a sole proprietorship without hiring an attorney. Even better, as the consultant and the owner of the consulting business, you have complete authority over all aspects of the business. Sole proprietors can operate any type of business on a full-time or part-time basis. Some sole proprietorship businesses include:

- Store or retail business
- Unincorporated company with one owner
- Home-based business
- Consulting firm with only one consultant

One of the major drawbacks of establishing your consulting business as a sole proprietorship is that you are personally liable for the business in all regards. If a client sues you for a business act, they can go after your personal assets. The business operator of a sole proprietorship is also personally liable for any loans or expenses of the company.

Sole proprietors are required to maintain company records that are in compliance with federal tax requirements for business records. This means they must file federal taxes using the Schedule C or C-EZ (Form 1040), Net Profit from Business, when they file their personal tax returns. The net business income or loss for a sole proprietor is included with any other revenue you receive and deductions you make. A sole proprietor is taxed at the individual tax rate on the personal tax return. Sole proprietors may choose to pay self-employment tax on the net income they claim using Schedule C. Sole proprietors may also be eligible to deduct half of the self-employment tax on Form 1040 using Schedule SE (Form 1040), Self-employment Tax, to calculate the amount of the tax. Sole proprietors do not have taxes withheld from their business income, so in order to make a profit it is typical for the sole proprietor to make quarterly tax payments, which are estimates based on the expected business income for the year and include income tax and self-employment taxes for social security and Medicare.

Partnership

A partnership forms when you share the ownership of your consulting business with at least one other person. The two most common forms of business partnerships are general partnerships and limited partnerships. While establishing a general partnership only requires an oral agreement, legal paperwork should be drawn up to make sure business items remain in order. The goal of a written agreement is to safeguard the business against problems and disputes that may arise between the partners of the consulting business. In a partnership, you and your partner are equally responsible for your own actions regarding business conduct and liabilities. There are some legal fees involved in creating the partnership agreement, although these costs are minimal and typically worth the investment.

A partnership is not required to pay income tax, but each individual partner is required to file Form 1065, U.S. Return of Partnership Income, to report the revenue and expenses for the partner. Form 1065 is an information form used to pass the information through to be included on the Schedule K-1, Partner's Share of Income, Credits, and Deductions, of the individual partners. Each partner then reports the net profit or loss of their portion of the partnership on personal tax returns (Form 1040). Similar to sole proprietors, partners usually make quarterly tax payments, which are estimates of the expected portion of the profit.

If you are the general partner in a partnership, then you are required by the IRS to pay a self-employment tax, which is calculated from your net income from the partnership. If you are a limited partner, you are required by the IRS to pay self-employment tax on the amount of income you receive for any services that you personally rendered to clients.

Corporation

A corporation is a business entity that stands on its own. Most consulting businesses do not start out as a corporation and most never become a corporation. When a consulting firm becomes a corporation, the businesses control is in the hands of the stockholders of the corporation. You do not need an attorney to incorporate your business but having legal advice to do so can help you avoid problems or difficult situations. Corporations cost more to organize and are much more complicated to set up than other forms of business, but it is possible to create a corporation that is less formal than larger corporations are. Corporate entities are required to keep organized and detailed written records, some of which have to be filed with the state where the corporation has its corporate headquarters. In terms of liability, the officers of the corporation are legally liable to the stockholders for any improper behavior or situations that may arise within business operations. This means that if the officers of a corporation do something that causes the business profits to go, which in turn affects the return on investment to stockholders in the company, then the officers are going to have to explain what caused the change and how they plan to correct the issue.

Shareholders of a corporation are responsible for paying tax on any dividends received from the corporation, which is reported on the shareholders' personal tax returns. The corporation is treated as an entity, so the corporation is responsible for paying taxes at the corporate tax rate. Corporations file tax Forms 1120 or 1120-A, U.S. Corporation Income Tax Return. If an employee of a corporation is also a shareholder of the corporation, then the employee is responsible for paying income tax earned as an employee for the company. The employee pays 50 percent of the social security and Medicare taxes charged on the amount of their income and the corporation is responsible for paying the other 50 percent.

S corporation

A subchapter S corporation is a type of corporation that permits the income or loss of the business to be passed through to individual tax returns of the business owners. Other than the way business income and loss is treated, a subchapter S corporation operates the same way a corporation does. Generally, an S corporation is treated similar to a partnership so it is not required to pay federal income tax, except specific capital gains and passive income. Rather than filing Form 1120 like general corporations, S corporations file Form 1120-S, U.S. Corporation Income Tax Return for an S Corporation. Each shareholder must complete Schedule K-1, Shareholder's Share of Income, Credits, and Deductions, which is included with Form 1120-S for each shareholder. The income is also reported on the shareholders' individual tax returns.

Limited Liability Company (LLC)

Another type of business setup is a limited liability company (LLC). An LLC possesses many of the same benefits that a corporation does. As a consultant, you will find that a LLC may be the most beneficial form of business because it limits your personal liability for company liabilities and legal issues. A LLC also offers you tax benefits that differ from a sole proprietorship or partnership consulting business, but an LLC does allow pass-through taxation.

Owners of a LLC are called members, which can be individuals, corporations, other LLCs and foreign entities. In some instances, a LLC only contains one member (one owner). Publication 3402, Tax Issues for Limited Liability Companies, available on the IRS website (**www.irs.gov**) provides specific information on the tax return forms LLCs must and how to handle employment taxes. In short, an LLC offers you more flexibility in your business setup and provides you with more options in how you can manage and operate your consulting business.

Governmental Requirements

Each state, county, and city in the United States has its own laws you must adhere to as well. You need to become familiar with the various requirements to establish your business legally and avoid future fines and problems from arising. This laws and regulations include everything from the zoning requirements where you can run your business and scheduling and passing required inspections to having the appropriate licenses and permits to run your business. The U.S. Business Advisor's website at **www.business. gov** provides helpful information to those looking to start a business, which includes:

- A business resource library
- Online counseling services
- Information on financial resources available to startup businesses
- Links to laws affecting different industries
- Legal and regulatory information for small businesses of all kinds

Plenty of other helpful tools are available to locate reliable information on starting a business.

- The Small Business Administration (**www.sba.gov/**) includes a list of consultants that service various industries and that provide a variety of services

- The IRS (**www.irs.gov**) helps prepare your business tax information and forms

- The U.S. Department of Labor (**www.dol.gov**) can help you manage employees and learn minimum requirements for working environments and other employment law and regulation information

Each state offers other resources from the state's department of business, which may also be called the state's Department of Development office.

One example of these helpful government-sponsored websites is Ohio's 1st Stop Business Connection (**http://development.ohio.gov/1stStop/OneStop/index.cfm**). This particular site is helpful because it offers step-by-step advice and instructions on creating your business. The business information kit includes forms, state regulations, and other tools to help answer questions of business entrepreneurs in Ohio. Each state offers similar advice and information kits for entrepreneurs starting business operations in the state. Other resources you can contact for assistance and to gather information is your local Economic Development Center, the chamber of commerce, or the Small Business Development Center. Call your local Equal Employment Opportunity Commission (EEOC) office as well, so you stay in compliance with any requirements they place on your business. For additional information and to locate local offices, visit **www.eeoc.gov**.

Your state's registration process

Contact your secretary of state's office to learn about the state requirements you have to meet for your business. This office will provide you with the laws with which you must comply in establishing and operating your business. The fee to register your business will vary by state. One of the main functions of the state office is to check to see if the business name you have selected is available or is already in use by another business operating in the state. Some states require you to file for and publish a fictitious name with the local newspaper before officially registering the name. Usually on an annual basis, the state requires you to renew the business name, but renewal times vary by state.

The state's department of taxation office can provide income tax information you need to be aware of for your business. This department supplies the necessary forms, tax tables, filing requirements, and publications to help you understand and meet tax-filing deadlines for the business. This information includes payroll deposit requirements for federal and state taxes, as determined by the type of your business, as well as federal and state unemployment deposit amounts and deadlines. Missing or not adhering to deadlines can earn your business expensive penalties, fines, and interest.

City business license

In most cities across the United States, you will need to register the business with the city where it operates. The city supplies a business license, which permits you to operate the business within the city limits. The county where your headquarters is located may also require a business license. If you work with clients in various cities, you may need to obtain a license in each of the cities where you have business before conducting business there. The fees associated with obtaining your business license vary by location. You can contact your local chamber of commerce to obtain the requirements and information you need to obtain your business license. If you are taking over an existing consulting firm, most states require that you apply for a license in your own name.

Sales tax

For states that charge and collect sales tax, even a consulting business, which is a service business, is required to collect and pay sales tax on the amount you charged the client for services rendered. For example, sales tax in Florida is 7 percent. If you charge a client $100 for a service, you also need to charge the client 7 percent sales tax on the $100. Each state's laws on the taxation of a sale are different, but you may need to obtain a vendor's license to collect sales tax, while other states may not require you to collect and pay sales tax at all. Sales taxes can be collected at the city, county, and state levels. The best place to find out what the sales tax requirements are for your business is to contact your state's department of taxation. The office and your state's website provide a variety of helpful resources. Some states require you to post a deposit on bond against possible future tax obligations; however, this may be waived if they require you to post a surety bond, which requires you to pay 5 percent of the total bond amount, from your insurance company instead. Your accountant and financial adviser can also advise you on the requirements your business has to meet.

Other Local Licenses and Requirements

Because each consulting business is unique or caters to a specific niche or industry, there may be other requirements you have to take care of before opening your business to the public.

Health department

If your consulting business deals with the sale of food, then another license you need to obtain is from the health department, and you will need to do this before opening your consulting business. With this license, you will be required to undergo periodic reviews from the health department to ensure you are meeting health standards. Contact the health department in your state or your county and they will guide you through the process of establishing your food-related consulting business correctly. You also have the option of visit the local office of the department of health to obtain the details and requirements for opening your business in conjunction with the law. If your consulting business does not abide by the health department's regulations, it may be shut down and prohibited from operating.

If you are required to obtain a license, the department conducts an inspection of your business location to ensure it is in compliance. Once your business fully passes this inspection, the department will issue your business a license. If there are any problems or issues that arise during the inspection, you will be given an opportunity to correct these issues before undergoing a follow-up inspection. If you pass the follow-up inspection then you are given a license. Keep in mind that food-related businesses usually receive unannounced visits to your business location to check to see if you are abiding by the health requirements. Any violations must be corrected within the time frame set, or you may lose your license.

Fire department

Another permit you need to be aware of is a fire permit. Typically, businesses with a location outside of the home are required to pass a fire safety inspection; however, even home-based consulting businesses that have special equipment or tools of the trade may be required to pass a fire inspection and obtain a fire permit. Contact your local fire department to see what the requirements are.

If you determine you have to undergo a fire inspection, the fire inspector will check your location's fire exits, fire extinguishers, smoke detectors, and sprinkler systems as they pertain to your business. They will evaluate the size of the location and the number of exits to determine the maximum capacity of the location as necessary. You must follow any guidelines they set in place for your location because failure to do so may result in fines, penalties, or the loss of your fire permit and ability to run your business in the location.

Construction and building

If you are going to remodel or build on your business's location, you are required to obtain a building permit before the construction work can begin. You can obtain building permits from your local building and zoning office (usually located in city hall). The building inspector may require a copy of your building or re-modeling plans and require the building to undergo an inspection before, during, and after the building commences. The final inspection of the building project includes a safety inspection of the footers, framing, insulation, electrical, plumbing, and other important elements of the building construction. You may also need to comply with appearance guidelines according to local requirements. Some cities require buildings to use some materials or approval of paint colors before the building is finished.

Sign permits

Some areas have laws to regulate the use of signs on buildings or on the street where the business is located. Signage requirements may cover the type, size, location, and lighting of the business sign you want to use for your business. According to county regulations and even the building regulations where your business is located, there are various sign requirements, including how high the sign can stand, how close to the business, and how close to the street it is. Before purchasing any type of sign for your business, check the city, county, and community codes where your business operates. For example, if you place a sign for your consulting business on the front lawn of your home, you may be charged a hefty fine for placing the sign in a residential community that does not permit business signs.

Zoning requirements

An area's zoning requirements dictate how buildings located in the zone can be used. For example, residential zoning allows for living while commercial zoning permits businesses to run out the location. Working out of your home is not typically affected by these zoning requirements, but check with your county permit department because some counties require you to obtain a home office permit. Some of the aspects of your business that can be affected by zoning requirements are where you can operate the business, where clients can park, and even what type of vehicles you can have in your driveway.

Employer identification number (EIN)

Even if you are a sole proprietor, you may wish to obtain an employer identification number (EIN) for your business, so you do not have to give your social security number to clients and vendors for income tax reporting purposes. If you are an employer, partnership, or a corporation, the IRS requires you to obtain an EIN for your business. This is the equivalent to a social security number but is used when filing your business tax forms, to open a business bank account, and to establish credit accounts for the business.

The process for obtaining an EIN for your business is relatively simple. The IRS's online application walks you through the process of requesting the number, and you can choose to obtain the number via e-mail or regular mail. You also have the option of downloading, printing, and completing a paper application directly from **www.irs.gov** or request a paper form be mailed to you. Finally, you can contact the IRS via phone and an IRS agent can process your application by phone.

Registering trademarks

When you use a word, phrase, symbol, or design that is special to your business, and you do not want another company to be able to use it, you can trademark the word, phrase, symbol, or design. You should only trademark items that in some way distinguish your company from any other business. The interesting thing about trademarks is that registering does not create your trademark; public use does. So, you are not required to file a trademark application with the United States Patent and Trademark Office (USPTO) in order to stake claim to the trademarked item. You can simply indicate your claim to the public by using the "TM" (trademark) symbol.

When and if you are ready to file a trademark application, you have a couple of different options on how to go about doing it. Your first option to complete the application online using the USPTO's Trademark Electronic Application System (TEAS) at **www.uspto.gov/teas**. This system allows you to complete and submit the trademark application directly over the Internet. You can also use the automated telephone line at 1-800-786-9199 to request a printed application. If you request a paper application, you must submit the application via regular mail or in person in the Alexandria, Virginia, office only.

Once you have your business structure in place and have obtained all of the necessary licenses and permits, you are ready and able to open for business. Once you are open for business, you have to learn how to properly manage your business revenue and expenses in order to run a profitable and successful consulting business.

☐ Checklist

☐	Decide which legal business structure is most beneficial to your business.
☐	Apply for and obtain any special permits or licenses you need in the state, county, and city where the business is located.
☐	Choose and register a business name and trademarks.
☐	Obtain a business or occupational license to operate your consulting business.
☐	Request and obtain an employer identification number (EIN).

Chapter 7

Managing Revenue
and Expenses

In this chapter, you will:

- Learn how to make projections on the revenue and expenses of the business.

- Discover bookkeeping and spending strategies to help create a profitable and legally compliant business.

- Uncover the secret ways you can keep expenses at a minimum, especially for the first few years of the business, until it starts to turn a profit.

Your business is well on its way to getting started, and you may already have landed a client or two. You are ready to jump right into the world of consulting, but managing your business is equally as important as the consulting work. The big obstacle that many consulting businesses face is how to set up their business bookkeeping or accounting records in an organized and efficient manner. Unfortunately, this is one aspect of getting your business up and running that can be one of the most difficult to organize. For this reason, learning how to handle the financial records of the business now can save you from a messy situation in the future.

The Business Budget

While your business plan includes a written estimate of your business budget you can use as a starting point, your business's life involves managing the budget you have put in place. Internal bookkeeping practices are an essential part of successfully running a business, and all financial transactions need to be recorded, reviewed, and balanced.

For consultants who are not mathematically inclined, it may behoove you to hire a professional accountant to handle these details of your business. When your business is first starting out, you can probably work with an accountant on a part-time basis. If you do decide to outsource this function, you still need to stay involved so you know and understand every financial detail as it pertains to your business's financial health. The faster potential problems are brought to light, the faster you can get these issues corrected and under control.

If you decide to be the financial manager of your own business, it may take you several hours daily (or at least weekly) to focus on and manage your business accounting. Luckily, accounting software programs are available and can be a helpful tool for keeping track of your books. Even if you conduct the accounting for your business, it is wise to have an accountant review your financial records on a quarterly basis to check for accuracy and offer advice on any adjustments that need to be made.

Accounting software

One of the best tools available to anyone starting a business is accounting software. There are many types available, though some are better suited to different types of consulting businesses than others. Nonetheless, the benefits of investing in the accounting software can far outweigh the cost of purchasing and implementing it.

Probably one of the most popular is Intuit QuickBooks® accounting software, which is specifically designed as a package with resources for small businesses. QuickBooks can help you with everything from managing inventory to keeping your profit and loss statement up to date. For certain business structures, QuickBooks even allows for electronic filing of the business federal tax returns. The software can be purchased in most office supply and computer software stores, as well as online on websites such as **http://quickbooks.intuit.com**. Pricing on the software starts at $229.95 for the most basic version and goes up to $600 for the most comprehensive versions, with enhanced reporting for up to three users and QuickBooks support service.

Another popular accounting software is Peachtree (**www. peachtree.com**) by Sage Accounting Software, which offers many benefits and features to you as a small business owner. Peachtree offers different versions of the software, so you have some flexibility in finding the version that is right for your business. For one to five users, the first three versions (Peachtree Pro, Peachtree Complete, and Peachtree Premium) are available. Peachtree

Quantum is the only version that allows more than five users. All versions offer standard accounting and management tools. The complete version also offers advanced inventory, job costing, an audit trail, and fixed assets tools. In addition, the premium version offers serialized inventory, Crystal Reports®, and advanced budgeting tools. Pricing ranges from $199.99 to $13,350, depending on the version and number of users that have access to the software.

These are but two of the many accounting software programs on the market. You can view and compare different software options at 2020software.com (**www.2020software.com**). The site lists the top-rated accounting software programs, see side-by-side comparisons of the various options, try out free demos, and speak with an accounting software specialist for additional help.

Payroll planning

If your consulting business has employees, even if you are the employee, it helps to understand the inner working of the payroll system of your business. In most cases, the process is simple for a one-consultant business, but in the case where there are multiple employees it is a more complicated process.

Bookkeepers can do payroll for your business by cutting the employee paychecks, making the required tax withholding deposits, and filing all of the necessary paperwork. An accounting software program such as QuickBooks or Peachtree also offers payroll features, which automates much of this work for you. A third option is to hire a professional payroll service to handle your payroll needs. In any of these situations, you will need to have a daily report prepared containing your daily accounts so you can provide employee information to your payroll accounting service for tracking data such as the salary or wages paid, deduction amounts for social security and Medicare taxes, and the number of hours worked if an hourly employee.

If you wish to allocate the time, your payroll service, bookkeeper, or accounting software program can do this for you as well. You can define the allocation categories and the hours spent on the project. This is especially helpful when you are charging clients on an hourly basis because clients want to see what they received for the fee they paid. Whether you choose a bookkeeper or accounting program to organize your business books, you can use this daily checklist to make sure your bookkeeping function is completed on a daily basis.

- Gather the number of hours worked by each employee (preferably as a written timecard).

- Verify the hours match the amount of time the employees worked.

- Record hours on payroll software or report it to your payroll service or bookkeeper.

- Determine the gross amount to be paid to each employee.

- For salaried employees, divide the employee's monthly salary by the number of days worked in the month (or divide the annual salary by 52 to determine a weekly salary amount).

- Total up the gross amounts for each day.

At the end of the week, total each employee's gross pay (your accounting software should do this for you). All records should be checked for accuracy. For example, if two employees are working on a large client project and you pay them hourly, you need to keep track of the hours the employees work in order to pay the employees and to track how much to charge the client. Preparing these figures on a daily basis helps you stay up to date on where your business stands financially. Reconciling this information with your budget can help you keep your business afloat.

Handling taxes

When it comes to dealing with business taxes, consulting businesses need to pay special attention to keeping accurate and up-to-date business records. Because consulting is typically a service business, it is more difficult for the IRS to track sales and expenses than it is for a product-based business. Therefore, the IRS is more likely to monitor service businesses on an effort to avoid tax fraud, so it is imperative to keep accurate records. One of the biggest issues with business taxes is determining how much you need to pay. With the various types of county, state, and federal taxes your business may be responsible for paying, there is no one calculation that applies to every business. One of the best places to start to get a handle on your business taxes is with the IRS; its website provides a myriad of information on resources on almost any tax matter you can think of occurring.

When it comes to federal business taxes, the three main categories you need to be concerned with paying and filing the appropriate forms are:

1. Income tax withheld from employees wages or from non-payroll amounts.

2. Social security and Medicare taxes (FICA taxes) from each employees' wages and the social security and Medicare taxes you pay as an employer.

3. Federal unemployment (FUTA) tax.

If you do not have any employees you may not have to worry about paying these taxes. Talk with your accountant or contact the IRS to determine if these taxes are applicable to your business. To file your business tax return, you may need access to the following forms:

*   **Form 940 (or 940-EZ), Employer's Annual Federal Unemployment (FUTA) Tax Return:** This form is due one month after the calendar year ends. Use it to report your FUTA tax. Most employers can use Form 940-EZ.

*   **Form 941, Employer's Quarterly Federal Tax Return:** File this one month after the calendar month or quarter ends. (The amounts of your payments dictate how often you need to file.) This form is used to report social security, Medicare, and federal income taxes withheld on your employees' wages.

Managing your cash

As you start working with clients, cash flow management comes into play. Your cash flow is the amount of money your company earns and spends during a certain time, and in order for your business to break even, you need to have enough cash flow to pay for bills, supplies, and other business expenses.

Managing your business cash flow accurately is crucial to running a successful business. It is good business practice for you to stay on top of your bills, so you always pay them on time. Doing so can often save you money, as some suppliers discount the amount you owe when you pay early or on time. Paying bills late, on the other hand, can cost you more because you will be charged late fees and finance charges on top of the amount you owe. In some situations, you will develop working relationships with suppliers and other vendors, which may afford you a 30-day window to pay your bill. This window allows you to leverage your cash flow, especially if your cash flow fluctuates during the month.

Managing cash flow comes down to inputting the payments you receive from clients into your accounting software as well as tracking the payments you are dispensing. It is similar to keeping a check register for your personal checking account. When you make a deposit, you place the deposit amount in the income column and add it to the total balance in your account. When you write a check, use your debit card, or withdraw cash from the account, you subtract the amount of money going out of the account from the balance. You keep track of the income and expenses going in and out of the account so you know how much money you have to spend and how much money you may need to earn in order to cover upcoming expenses. The same concept holds true for managing the cash flow in your consulting business.

CASE STUDY: THE VALUE OF SPREADSHEETS

The Collaborative and Advisors
Trusted Advisor
Beverly Flaxington
Medfield MA 02052
508-359-8216
www.the-collaborative.com and
www.advisorstrustedadvisor.com

Beverly Flaxington runs two consulting businesses, both of which focus on business building, helping firms to gain more revenue and understand their internal obstacles to success. Then she helps them create a plan to remove the obstacles and implement the plan. The Collaborative is a broader sales, marketing, and training firm. The second business, Advisors Trusted Advisor, has an exclusive focus in the investment industry.

When it comes to managing the income and expenses of the businesses, Flaxington's biggest obstacle has been tracking specific expenses against a project or a client. Her businesses handle so many different things that they often do not take the time to connect back the expenses to specific situations. While they have a general idea where the expense originated, they do not track a P&L for each effort. The income side is the variability — sometimes the businesses are overwhelmed with income and work, and then the business may hit a lull.

In order to overcome this, Flaxington has learned to "bank" much of the income from her businesses during the good times, which helps them function during leaner times. They also continually focus on selling and marketing, which has helped to minimize — if not eliminate — the lean times altogether. The businesses recently instituted a program where all of the staff updates a spreadsheet with information such as hours and expenses for each client and project as they occur, which she feels will help with tracking the client expenses and ultimately their P&L in a more effective manner.

Accepting Client Payments

One of the factors you need to consider is the types of payments you will accept from clients. You can choose to accept cash, checks, money orders, cashier's checks, and debit and credit cards. Determining which type of payments you accept from clients also affects your cash flow. For example, if you choose to accept only checks then you simply have to cash or deposit the check into your business bank account. You will only be charged fees on the check if for some reason it bounces.

There are a couple of disadvantages to accepting checks. First, you have to wait to receive the check from the client, either in person or by mail. This can cause a delay in your receipt of the payment. Second, you have to make a trip to the bank to deposit it into your account, and if the check is from an out-of-state bank or over the bank's limit amount, the funds may be put on hold, which means you will not have immediate access to the money. Third, if the check bounces because the client does not have sufficient funds in his or her bank account, your bank may charge bounced check fees; this may even cause checks you have written from your bank account to bounce, which can result in even more bounced check fees for you to pay.

If you choose to accept credit cards, on the other hand, you are typically charged a percentage of the transaction as a fee. The percentages can range from 2 percent of the transaction amount to more than 3 percent. There are typically transaction fees as well, so each time you run a credit card for payment, not only are you charged the percentage of the transaction amount, but you also pay a flat rate fee, which can range from 30 cents up. Instead of receiving 100 percent of the client payment, you walk away with the amount left after the credit card processing fee is deducted. Because there are various ways you can receive payments from clients, consider the pros and cons of each option — including the costs — before deciding which forms of payment you should accept for your business. Here are some of the payment options you can consider accepting from clients:

- **Cash:** Be sure to provide the client with a receipt signed by you and the client when you accept this form of payment. A signed receipt is your only record of the transaction.

- **Checks:** Personal or business checks have some risk because they may bounce, but you typically do not pay fees for cashing or depositing checks into your business account. Be sure to charge a fee for any returned checks (and record that fee amount at the time of billing).

- **Credit and debit cards:** Accepting credit and debit payments is convenient, and with instant approval or denial you have a sense of security that the money is available. Clients like to pay with credit cards because it allows clients to pay off the charge down the line.

- **Online:** Online payment processing programs such as PayPal and Google Checkout allow you to accept credit card or check payments online, which speeds up the payment process. Again, there is a fee for using these services, but it is typically less expensive than having a credit card machine. The fee charged is a percentage of the transaction amount, but typically starts at 1 percent of the transaction amount and goes up to slightly more than 2 percent, depending on the type of credit card the client uses and the account level you have established with PayPal or Google Checkout.

Tips for accepting cash and checks

When using cash, keep these things in mind:

- **Trust the cash collector:** If you are entrusting the collection of cash to someone in your business other than you, it is imperative that the person collecting the cash is reliable and honest. Making one person responsible for collecting and managing the cash makes it easier to track mistakes, mishaps, or theft.

- **Keep detailed records:** All cash transactions should be recorded with details on the exact amount paid, when the cash payment was received, and exactly what the payment covers (which services).

- **Generate a cash receipt:** The client and the person in your business accepting the payment should sign this receipt. Include detailed information such as the payment amount, date, and reason for the payment.

- **Balance the cash drawer:** The cash drawer should be balanced on a regular basis and excess amounts should be deposited in the bank. Businesses that have a high amount of cash transaction balance the cash drawer and make deposits on a daily basis. Those with a less cash volume business may only do this once a month.

When using checks, keep these things in mind:

- **Include a returned check fee:** In the terms section of the client contract or agreement, spell out the fee that will be charged to clients for any returned checks.

- **Include all contact information for the payee:** On the check, include an address, phone number, and business name (if appropriate). Verify this information for an individual against a picture ID before accepting a check as payment. This information can help to avoid accepting fraudulent checks and help you to track down the client for payment in the event the check bounces or you have some other problem with depositing or cashing the check.

- **Generate a receipt:** Create a receipt for check payments and have the client sign it. Include the amount of the payment, the date of the payment, and the reason for the payment.

- **Consider using a check confirmation system:** These systems verify that there is money available in the account from which the check is written at the time you take the check. The system can place the funds on hold until the check clears. This can be an expensive service, but it can also be beneficial when accepting a check from a client for the first time. Contact your bank for more information on the cost of this system and how to implement it.

Contracts and payments

In the world of consulting, you will find that most clients pay with a check, but you can set the proper payment expectations with the client when the client contracts your services.

Make sure that each client contract outlines specific dates or milestones that trigger a payment and how much is due for each payment. Because you will most likely spread the payments out into several stages, your first step is to request an upfront payment or deposit to start the project. This provides you and the client with a sense of security. You know that you are working on a project that the client has a vested interest in, so you do not end up working for free. The client has received assurance that he or she has booked your time and services in advance. It is less likely that a client will walk away from a project when they have given you a deposit or upfront payment.

Collecting payments is a give-and-take situation between you and the client. When you reach certain milestones, the client receives a report from you and in return you receive a portion of the total fee. For example, if you establish a four-part payment arrangement with a client, then 25 percent of the payment is made at the start of the project, another 25 percent is paid when 50 percent of the work is done, 25 percent is paid when three-quarters of the project is done, and the final 25 percent is paid when the project is complete. This helps to provide you with a steady revenue flow as you begin to complete the project without having to wait until the end to get paid.

With retainer clients or clients you work with on a regular basis, you can set a regular payment schedule where you invoice them on a weekly or monthly basis. Whatever the agreement is, make sure the details are in your contract.

Your Budget and Operational Management

As part of any normal business operation, setting a realistic budget and then sticking to it can make a huge difference in a business succeeding or failing. This requires you to assess your budget situation before making any business purchases or investments to make sure the business can afford to do so. When creating a business budget, you will probably have two budgets that work in conjunction with each other. One deals with short-term expenses such as office supplies and the business phone bill, while the other deals with long-term financial plans for the business such as expanding your office space to accommodate more employees.

At least once a year, analyze your business needs and examine the costs associated with your business. When reviewing your business revenue and expenses, compare the actual amount spent with the amount that was budgeted for. This analysis helps you to see where you have shortfalls or overspending habits and helps you to allocate money better in the future. When there is a discrepancy between these numbers, find out what factors contributed to the discrepancy. Assessing the budget on a regular basis makes it easier to adjust and accommodate the costs now rather than waiting six months to find out your business is not generating enough income.

For your short-term budgeting practices, develop a monthly budget for the business. The first month you are in business may be more challenging to calculate costs than the months that follow, and it may take you a couple of months to truly understand what expenses your business has so that you can create a realistic budget. Over time, setting the monthly budget will become easier and probably more accurate. Creating and using a monthly budget as a guide for your business reveals how much money you can use for various expenses throughout the month. Ultimately, this budget helps you define where your business is going and what adjustments may need to occur in order to achieve your business goals. Keeping track of your budget can also be helpful when and if you apply for a business loan, as well as make it possible to meet your business financial goals. Accounting software programs have budgeting tools that allow you to create and keep track of your spending.

Building a budget out one month at a time can be accomplished with a spreadsheet or a piece of paper and a pencil. Choose the way you feel most comfortable in creating and tracking your budget. A budget boils down to a list of expenses and the estimated amounts for each expense. Once you list out all of the expenses, you can total them up to see what the total expenses are for the month.

Creating a budget is about estimating costs, so one column of your budget should list the actual amount paid out. Once you compare the expected expense with the actual expense, you can see if you need to adjust your estimates up or down, or keep them where they are. A budget for the month may contain five columns. Column one is the date of the expense, column two is the type of expense (phone service, office rent, or electricity), column three is estimated amount, column four is the actual amount paid, and the final column is the difference, if any, between the estimated amount of the expense and the actual amount of the expense.

Making revenue projections

Not only is it important to track the spending in your business, but it is also equally important to project your sales or the amount of revenue coming into the business. The best way to do this is to track earnings as you start to do business with a client. In addition, it is important to factor in that your earnings will probably be lower when you first start your consulting business, but as time progresses, you should start to earn more. With less money coming into the business and high one-time, startup expenses in the beginning, you will probably see a lower profit margin for the business and for you. In some situations, you may break even or lose money during the first few months in business. Tracking the profit margin for each service can also play a starring role in turning a business profit. If it costs you too much to use specific software to work on a client project and you are not turning a high enough profit on the service, then it may not be worth investing in the software. In that case, you would have to find another way to accomplish the client project without the software. Another option is to increase the service fee you charge to the client, but this can lead to you losing the client altogether. Either way, it is important that you track the profit margins on your services because you want to only work on projects that are bringing profits to your consulting company.

Part of being in a business is starting off slow and watching the revenues of your business grow over time. Growing your business requires you to project the business revenue and then track it to make sure it is actually growing. If business revenues hit a peak or a plateau, it is imperative that you understand what caused the peak, plateau, or plummet so you can make adjustments to either mimic it or make it better. For example, a seasonal business such as a wedding consulting firm may hit a peak during the spring and summer months when weddings are plentiful. Another example may be that a special promotion creates a spike in sales. On the other hand, off-peak wedding season such as the dead of winter in the northeast region of the country or the sweltering summer month of August in the south may create a plummet in revenues. Knowing what may be causing these swings is important because it can help you understand what is affecting the business profitability.

It is important to continuously track and compare your current revenue month by month, quarter by quarter, and year by year. Review these records often to compare the services, discounts, client base, and any other factors that may contribute to rise or fall in these numbers.

The Costs of Doing Business

The costs of doing business can vary greatly from company to company. One type of consulting company may have very little overhead or low expenses, while another consulting company has a huge overhead and more expenses than income. For example, a marketing consultant who works out of a home office has very little overhead. A landscaping consultant who has expensive design software, the tools and machinery (lawnmowers, shrub trimmers, shovels) to turn their design creations into a reality, the truck and trailer to haul all of the equipment, and a storage place for the equipment when it is not in use has much more overhead and expenses. As a business owner, you have to track all of your business expenses and revenue. First, you need to know and understand some of the business costs you may run up against so you can factor these costs into your budget. Some of the costs will not apply to your business, while other costs not listed here may apply to your type of consulting business. This is why factoring a cushion of money into your budget for emergencies and other unexpected expenses is important.

Labor costs

Labor is the cost of hiring employees. This includes everyone from the person selling your services to the person managing your front office. If you have employees, you need to know how much it is costing your business to have them on staff. When labor costs get too high, you can cut back on the number of employees. Conversely, you can hire additional help when needed. The number of employees you have on the payroll should be justified by the amount of business the employees are generating.

Perhaps one of the highest costs in terms of labor is overtime. When you have an employee who works more than 40 hours a week, you end up paying him or her 1½ times the amount of his or her normal rate. It is less expensive, in most cases, to hire an additional employee or to outsource the work instead of paying an employee to work extra hours.

Controllable operational costs

Controlling business costs, especially when you first start your business, is the key to keeping expenses low and helping to make your profit margin higher. With controllable costs, you can either choose to spend money on these costs or not, thus giving you more leeway with your expenses. Even if you decide to spend the money, you can still control how much an expense it becomes for your business. Here is a brief look at some of the business expenses you can control:

Large purchases: When you first start a business, there are likely to be larger purchases to acquire the equipment, furniture, and other supplies you need to start your business. While a purchase may be necessary, there are ways you can keep these costs down. For example, if you need to purchase a desk for your office, consider secondhand stores where you can find gently used furniture at a deep discount. You can also shop furniture sales, garage sales, and scour Craigslist (**www.craigslist.org**) ads for a desk. Another option to keep costs down is to repurpose items you already have to fit your needs. Instead of purchasing a new desk, consider using a table you have until you can afford to purchase a desk. You can also borrow items from friends and family members.

Service staples: Even though as a consultant you provide a service, there are supplies that you may need to purchase and keep on hand in order. For example, if you are an accounting consultant, you may need to acquire accounting software licenses in order to set up an accounting software program for each of your clients at their office. Because this is a cost for a specific product, you need to factor it in to your costs on an ongoing basis. Office supplies are another category that may fall into the staples category. Everything from printer paper and specialty paper to pens, folders, and paper clips can fall into this category. Because these types of items are consumables, you will need to replace them often. Keeping an inventory of your office supplies can help you reduce costs in the long run. You can opt to shop discount office supply stores online, which is less expensive than shopping bigger chain office supply stores — even with shipping.

Services: Your business may require some professional service providers, such as an attorney and accountant. Other services may not be as important. If you cannot afford to hire an accountant or payroll service, then consider lower-cost options such as purchasing and maintaining an accounting software program to help you with this aspect of your business. Also think along the lines of your shipping services when cutting costs or trying to keep operational costs to a minimum. For example, if you are sending a client a proposal, decide if you really need to print it out, put it in a company folder, and pay for it to go overnight to the client or if e-mailing the proposal is an effective, faster, and less expensive way to go.

Maintenance costs: Other operational costs include the maintenance of your office, equipment, company vehicles, and other machines you may own or lease for your business. These costs may include repair costs or fees for the upkeep on the materials to keep everything in working order. It is also important to consider that paying for maintenance fees can save you replacement costs on the equipment, so you do not want to disregard the maintenance altogether.

Utilities: Whether you run your consulting business at another location or in your home, utility costs for water and electricity are necessary operational costs. If you are running the business from its own location, utility costs will probably be higher than the small increase you may see when running your business out of your home. Other utility costs may include telephone, Internet service, and gas. You can keep costs down by only subscribing to those services that are necessary to run your business. For example, phone service packages may include a myriad of features that you do not need. Check with the phone company to see how much you can save if you only have the features you need such as call waiting and voice mail service.

Operating an energy-efficient business can also save you money on your utility bills. When machines, equipment, and lights are not in use turn them off and unplug them from the power source where applicable. When you close your business for the day, make sure you turn everything off. If you leave your computer for more than ten minutes, place it in sleep mode or set it up so that it automatically goes into sleep mode after it is dormant for a certain amount of time.

Fixed operating costs

While you may be able to control the amount you spend on some operational costs, other costs of running your consulting business are fixed costs, which mean the costs do not change from one payment cycle to the next. Fixed costs are also included as part of your business operational budget and can be easier to manage because the cost does not change.

Rent/mortgages: Whether you rent or own the property where you run your business, your rent or mortgage payment is the same month after month. This will be one of the first fixed costs that you will want to pay off each month so you ensure you still have a location to run your business.

Insurance costs: Liability insurance is a necessity when running a consulting business, so at the very least your insurance fixed cost covers this type of coverage. Depending on where your business location is (in or out of your home) you may have other insurance costs. Typically, insurance payments remain the same for long periods of time. Liability, theft, fire, and worker's compensation are a few types of insurance you may want to consider or may be required by law to obtain. Theft and fire insurance cover you in the event you lose your ability to run your office because of burglary or fire damage. Some policies offer you coverage for establishing a temporary office, while others only cover you for returning your existing office to its original condition. If you have employees on staff, worker's compensation can protect you in case of an employee injury. The insurance covers the cost of the employee's medical needs and can also protect you by paying the damages from a lawsuit brought on by the employee.

Property taxes: Property tax is another fixed cost that tends to come due once a year. If you are running your business out of your home, this should not affect the cost of your taxes. If you own a business location outside of your home, the county assesses a property tax value that you must pay at least once a year.

Miscellaneous costs

Other costs you need to consider and be aware of for running your consulting business include:

Labor taxes: If, or when, you have employees on the payroll, you will be responsible for paying taxes to the state and federal governments. Paying labor taxes requires you to establish an account with your business banking institution to deposit withholding amounts from each payroll period. These taxes typically include state and federal unemployment and social security.

Repair costs: Repairs for equipment, a company vehicle, or office location are unexpected costs that you may have to manage as well. Because these are unexpected expenses, keep a cushion of extra cash on hand to cover repair costs.

Client entertainment: Because you will be working with clients, there will be times when you need to woo them with a nice lunch, dinner, or tickets to the local sports game. Build some money into your budget to cover these types of client entertainment expenses and keep track of your spending because most of these items are tax deductible.

Advertising: Marketing and promoting your business typically requires quite a bit of your business budget — especially when you first launch the business. Once you complete your marketing plan in Chapter 10, you will have a better idea how much these expenses can run. Remember though, if nobody knows your business exists then it is going to be very difficult to attract clients and extremely difficult to stay in business.

Fees: Many consulting businesses have to pay trade dues or business association fees, which also needs to be taken into consideration when building your business budget. Also, the fees for obtaining and renewing the necessary business and occupational licenses should be allotted to this portion of your budget.

Client costs: There will be times when you need to travel to meet with a client, or you need to book a meeting room, and these costs also need to be taken into consideration. When possible, costs of this nature should be paid by the client and established in your written agreement, but you may initially need the cash on hand to cover the costs until receiving payment from the client.

Bad debt: Although you may do everything in your power to avoid it, there are times when a client project simply goes bad or takes a wrong turn. A client may disappear on you without paying you everything they owe, or you may underestimate a project that ends up costing more than you are getting. These types of instances are losses to your company that adversely affect your profit margin. Some of these losses may be tax deductible, but some come directly out of your budget, so keep track of these losses. For example, the interest you pay on business credit card balances is not a tax-deductible debt. If you carry large credit card balances, you are most likely paying interest that reaches into the double digits, and all of the interest you are paying is an added expense that you cannot write off as a business expense at the end of the year.

Calculating profit or loss

Once you keep a running tab of your income and your expenses, it is pretty easy to calculate your profit (or loss). Using all of the figures — keeping track of costs, expenses, and client payments — you simply subtract all of your costs and expenses from the total amount of money your services have brought into the company (revenue). When you subtract your expenses from your income, if the number is positive, then you have a profit. When you subtract your expenses from your income, if the number is negative then you have a loss. If and when you have a profit, decide how much of the company profit you will use to pay for your salary as opposed to how much of the profit will be reinvested back into the business. For example: Assume you are calculating profit and loss for the month of February, and the total monthly expenses are $2,575 and the total monthly income is $5,250.

Monthly profit: $5,250 – $2,575 = $2,675

In cases where the number is positive, this indicates a profit (more money was made than was spent). If the answer of the calculation is a negative number, this indicates a loss (more money was spent than was made).

CASE STUDY: THE TIME
CHALLENGES YOU MAY FACE

InnovationLabs LLC
Michael Kaufman
Walnut Creek, CA 94595
510-903-0652
www.innovationlabs.com

InnovationLabs designs and facilitates large group planning processes — or innovation labs — in which weeks, months, or years of work are completed in a matter of days. Clients come from every industry and segment of the economy and society including Fortune 500 corporations, foundations, government agencies, educational institutions, startups, and community-based organizations. Cofounder Michael Kaufman and the other partners of the consulting firm often work with multi-stakeholder groups that cut across an entire industry or segment. The niche is in facilitated planning processes and increasing the innovation capability of organizations and groups.

When it comes to managing the income and expenses of the business, the biggest challenge in consulting is an old adage that is called the "hunter/skinner syndrome." It refers to the time and energy it takes to hunt clients versus the time and energy it takes to skin (serve) those clients takes. Very large consulting firms have a model where everyone is a "hunter," but the "skinning" is performed by junior consultants who are billed at a lower rate than senior consultants. Kaufman has never liked this model and has attempted to have senior consultants — or partners — procure and service the engagement. The weakness in that model is the pipeline of business is not always full, and there can be many months of no work for one or several of the partners.

The other challenge is scheduling. This comes from the perception of the client on whether he or she in an industry that is rapidly changing. Because every organization is technically operating in a rapidly changing environment — although, some companies and industries have not figured this out yet — organizational structures tend to keep these organizations moving slowly and as if they have all the time in the world.

For instance, a software company knows it is in an extremely competitive and rapidly changing environment, so it has tremendous pressures to deliver quickly. It might realize that it needs to move faster — and possibly even that it is in a catch-up mode — so it wants to schedule something immediately and get the work done now — no matter how much work needs to be done.

Foundations, educational institutions, government agencies, and non-profits have a legacy of being structured as if they are in a less pressured and competitive environment. They might schedule something 12 months from now and then think they have three years to implement what they come up with.

Kaufman and the InnovationLabs partners have learned many lessons from these obstacles, which led them to redesign their process to be "transportable" so they could take it on the road. Now they ship and build a physical planning environment that is creative and innovative. They have processes in place that allow for very fast responses (within a week or two) and have other processes in place that allow for longer-term project management. Because they work with large groups of people, their work has been the best marketing tool for their business. Most engagements lead to other engagements, and that often takes care of the pipeline issue.

☐ Checklist

☐	Project and create a budget on expected revenue and expenses for the business.
☐	Research the possibilities of how you will handle your business financials.
☐	Build in cost-saving measures while building your budget but also create a cushion for emergencies and unexpected expenses.
☐	Track all of your revenue and expenses, and calculate whether your business is operating at a profit or loss.

Chapter 8

How to Manage Your
Time and Yourself

In this chapter, you will:

- Learn time management skills and tips on how to make the best use of your time.

- Discover how to balance your time so that you devote enough time to being a business owner, as well as handling client projects.

- Decide when and if it is time to delegate certain aspects of the business to others.

One of the primary requirements of running a successful consulting business goes beyond your knowledge and experience in the industry or niche you serve. You also have to learn how to be a prosperous business owner. Finding the right balance between devoting time to your role as a business owner and as a consultant can be challenging because both roles can literally be full-time jobs. Finding the balance really comes down to learning how to effectively manage your time, which also entails learning how to manage yourself in the process.

Time is Money

As a business owner, you no longer have a boss to monitor your time and task completion because you are the boss. There is no one looking over your shoulder to keep you on schedule or to make sure the company is heading toward achieving its goals. You are in charge, which means you are the only one accountable for the hours you work and for the work getting done. For most consultants who are also business owners, this is the most difficult challenge they have to overcome.

While you have the ability to spend countless hours at your desk working away or decide to call it a day at 2 p.m., the first thing you have to realize is that time is money. By learning to manage your time, you can also effectively manage the amount of money you will make while delivering the high quality of service you want to provide to your clients (and the paycheck to match all of your efforts). If you are not able to organize and manage your time effectively, you may end up wasting precious time, which also equates to wasting money before you have an opportunity to earn it.

CASE STUDY: AVOID
PROCRASTINATION WITH TO-
DO LISTS

The Geisheker Group Marketing Firm
Peter Geisheker
Green Bay, WI 54304
920-471-1638
www.geisheker.com

The Geisheker Group Marketing Firm provides marketing and advertising services for small and medium-sized businesses. After doing marketing for a company, Peter Geisheker, the firm's founder, realized that once you have a great marketing system in place, keeping it going is not a full-time job. He decided he could provide high-quality, results-driven marketing services for several companies at the same time and earn far more money doing that than by being an employee. Timing his transition worked perfectly because the company Geisheker worked for as an employee hired him to manage their marketing program and became his first client. From there, he acquired a couple more clients through local networking clubs.

Time and self-management tools and strategies are a consultant's best friends. Peter Geisheker makes a to-do list of the five most important things he needs to get done each day. He focuses on getting those items done. He believes that if you do not force yourself to create a to-do list that you religiously follow, you will find yourself wasting most of your day checking e-mail, surfing the Web, and doing things that are not conducive to growing your business. As a consultant, you must have strong self-discipline to get projects done in a timely manner. If you do not force yourself to work and you let procrastination run your life, you will quickly go out of business. Procrastination is your enemy, and it will do everything it can to kill your business.

Managing your time wisely

Setting priorities is the first step in learning how to manage your time wisely. Every client thinks that his or her project is more pressing or more important than one of the other client projects you have on your plate. Do not look to your clients to guide you on what to set as a priority over something else. You have to define what your priorities are, even if it means telling a client — in the nicest way possible — that you are unable to deal with their problem right now because you have something else you have to do. If you allow others to control your priorities, you end up not completing the important items, which over time can lead to a loss of business, money, and time.

As a consultant, you will have what may be or what seem like an endless demand for your attention. You have to balance meeting the demands of your clients to keep them happy with performing revenue-generating tasks to turn a profit. When setting your priorities for the day, there are several things to consider. Once you take these items in consideration, it will become much clearer on the order your tasks should fall.

1. **Is the task profitable?** Tasks that generate the most revenue for your business directly or indirectly are priorities. The bigger the payoff is, the higher the task should be on your lost. For example, if you have the choice of working on your marketing plan or heading out to the store to buy the new BlackBerry® phone, then working on your marketing plan should take priority. While putting together a marketing plan may not make you $1,000 today, it is a task that can make your company more profitable over time. On the contrary, tasks that have less of an impact on your profitability should be toward the bottom of your task list, such as administrative tasks like filing or tackling long-term projects like redesigning the business's website.

2. **Is it something you should handle or delegate to someone else?** Many business owners get caught up in the fact that they are the only ones who can do something right, so they may as well handle everything. Highly effective and successful people quickly learn that the true way to make it to the top is to build a great support team, either as employees or as independent contractors. This allows the business owner to focus on profit-generating activities and delegate tasks that someone else has the ability to handle. Delegation can propel you toward meeting your business goals faster than getting bogged down with everything and getting nothing accomplished in the process.

3. **Are you the emergency room doctor?** What clients often think is an emergency and what is truly an emergency typically are two different things. As the emergency room doctor, it is up to you to decide. If it is a real problem that needs handling immediately, then move it toward the top of your priority list. For example, if your largest client's server goes down and he is losing money, you need to get that server up and running before moving on to the next client's project. Build some time into your daily schedule in case emergencies arise so it does not completely throw off your entire schedule.

As projects come in, use this three-step approach to determine the priority level of the project. As you complete a project, move to the next top priority on your list. Some days you will get through your entire list. Other days, you may not get past the first item on your task list. Continue to plan each day using your list, rearranging items in order of importance. Prioritize your list for the day according to the deadlines that need to be met for each task.

Eight effective time-management tips

Managing your time and your effectiveness starts with knowing what your goals are and how to meet them. These eight tips will help you to get on the right track to managing your time.

Tip 1: Always be in the know

The first place to start is with a list of projects and tasks that need to be tackled. While these items may not be in order just yet, you always need to know what needs to be done and have a big-picture view. You must always have all of the information you need at your fingertips; therefore, you must always be organized. If you work best with a hard-copy day planner that you carry around, then use this as your task system. If a computerized calendar or spreadsheet of projects and tasks is what works to keep you organized, then use this system to keep track of everything. Find an organizational system that works for you, and then learn how to manage it rather than allow it to manage you.

Tip 2: Start off the day right

Each morning when you start your workday, pull out your schedule/task list or pull up your goals on the computer. Because your tasks should be in order of priority, you can start to tackle the most important item on your list and work your way down the list as you complete each task. As you progress through the day, you will also find yourself adding items to your list. Work these items in according to priority. If the task is more important than an item already on the list, then insert the new item above the existing items that are less important. If the new item is less important, add it to the bottom of the list

Tip 3: End the day right

At the end of each workday, set some time aside to prepare and organize the schedule for the following day. Review the current day's task list, and assess what you were able to accomplish and what items on the list need to be moved to the following day. Prepare the plan, task list, and schedule for the following day, so that when you start work the following day, you are ready to get started right away. It may also be beneficial to save administrative tasks such as invoicing and filing for the end of the day because this is the time when you are typically getting tired. Clean off your desk so it is fresh and clean when you arrive tomorrow, turn off your lights and computer, and end your workday on an organized note.

Tip 4: Tackle your first priority first

Make sure that you are handling your daily tasks according to the priority set for them. It may sound simple, but the first priority is often a difficult task or project, so consultants tend to avoid handling it and instead focus on smaller, less difficult, and less important tasks. Consultants often rationalize that getting all of the little things off their plate allows them to focus on what is important. The opposite, however, ends up being the case. Yes, all of the smaller items may be crossed off the list of things to accomplish, but the priority item is still staring them in the face — unaccomplished and incomplete. Projects with looming deadlines, matters with a sense of urgency, and problems need to be handled first. After that, you can focus on less important items.

If the task list has 25 items on it, you probably are not going to accomplish everything on your list in one day. It is fine not to get through your list in an entire day as long as you have set your priorities correctly.

Tip 5: Cut out tasks that are not lucrative

Focus your efforts for the bulk of the day on tasks that are lucrative and make the consulting business money. This includes marketing tasks, completing client projects, and preparing proposals for new clients. Checking and responding to e-mails, filing, and playing with the calendar are less lucrative tasks. While these are tasks that need to be done, schedule a set time to tackle these tasks and then stick to your schedule. The more time you spend on activities that do not generate income, the less time you have for finding new clients, working on meeting deadlines, and making money. Instead of reading blogs for the first hour of your workday, spend that time networking to find your next client, and save blog reading for the end of the day.

It can also be helpful to filter e-mails coming in through your e-mail system so that specific client e-mails are easily accessible, and all of the spam and promotional e-mails are placed in a folder that you can access at a more convenient time, if ever.

Tip 6: Use your time wisely

As a consultant, there may be down time throughout the day when you are not working on a client project or attempting to complete a lucrative task. Other down times include waiting at the airport to catch a flight to meet with a client or sitting in the taxi on the way to a meeting. Rather than let these times go waste, take along work that can be completed during the ride in the cab, sitting in the airport terminal, and while on the airplane. Networking opportunities may also present themselves during travel of this nature, so talk to the people sitting around you at the airport and on the plane and hand out business cards when appropriate. You never know where your next client will come from.

Tip 7: Technology is your friend

Technology can be a useful and helpful tool for a consulting business because it allows you to make wise use of time. Because time is money, properly utilizing technology can be very lucrative for a consulting business. Using an iPhone®, BlackBerry, or another smart phone can help consolidate your technological needs into one instrument. These devices are a phone, calendar, e-mail system, word processing system, and task creator all wrapped up in one convenient package — and with Internet access.

Investing in a laptop rather than a desktop computer may be a wiser option for consultants who are always on the go rather than always in the office. Software programs are available for consultants to maximize their time by handling certain administrative tasks. E-mail correspondence can replace the cost of physical mail or long distance phone charges. Instant messaging conversations can also replace other forms of communication as a fast, easy, and cost-effective way to get things done. Use the business website to automatically gather business leads. Technology is a consultant's most powerful tool, making your business better and helping you grow the bottom line.

Tip 8: Build a cushion of time

When planning a schedule, try not to plan out a task for every minute of the day. While it is good to have tasks scheduled, everyone needs a break. Take a 15-minute break in the morning and afternoon, and be sure to take time for lunch, too. One consultant who works from home eats her lunch and then takes her dog for a quick 20-minute walk around the block. It helps clear her head and exercise the dog at the same time. When she returns to her desk, she has a clearer view of the work before her.

When the afternoon laziness sets in, work on activities that do not require too much brainpower or tackle administrative work. Building in a cushion of time also helps when urgent matters arise because it allows you to allocate what may have been some down time to resolving the problem without having to take too much time away from your other priorities. Time management is one of the most beneficial skills a consultant can have. It builds a thriving business, saves you from having to work hard to keep your head above water, and is a completely free tool.

Create an action plan

Professional service providers, with consultants being at the top of the list, have to possess or learn organizational skills in order to run a successful business. Organization is required, not optional, in the consulting industry. Being organized goes beyond knowing where you put a client contract or where the invoice is that you need to send to a client. Being organized is having the ability to find everything you need quickly and efficiently. Organization helps you to manage clutter and easily reach for what you need, but it is also an effective tool for managing your stress level.

While you may not realize it, a messy desk or messy office is counterproductive — even if you are not a neat freak. A messy desk is likely to have sticky notes, piles of paper, and other unnecessary or unused junk. The phone rings and a client asks a question that requires you to find a study you printed. As you rummage through the stacks of paper on your desk trying to find the study, it is easy for the client to see that you are distracted or cannot put your finger on the study itself. In addition to seeming unprofessional, clutter and disorganization make you feel less in control. Choose an organizational system you like and that works for you and then stick to it.

Getting the office organized and establishing a business system takes a commitment and time. You may want to set aside one full day, or at least a couple of hours, to organize and get your business system in place before you launch your business. Once you establish the organizational system, maintaining it requires your commitment and dedication. Maintaining an established system is much easier than the initial setup, however.

1. **Start with the desk:** It is easy for a work desk to become crowded with papers, documents, and other office supplies. The good news is that a desk can quickly be cleaned and stay that way. First, throw away any unused items and remove items from the desk that are not work related. If keeping paper files, find a filing cabinet and set up a filing system for invoices, contracts, expenses, long-term clients, and other business needs. Every piece of paper should have a home, and the desk surface is not a home. The surface of the desk and desk drawers should be clean, organized, and contain business items.

2. **Analyze the layout of the office:** Even an office of a couple hundred square feet can have an efficient, organized, and clean setup. Whether your office is your guest bedroom or a section of the dining room, analyze the space available as well as the furniture and equipment that goes in the space. After removing anything from the space that is not business related, arrange everything so it fits comfortably and is appealing to look at and work in. Rearrange everything until all necessary items have a home.

3. **Scheduling time and appointments:** Everyone uses different techniques to keep track of a calendar and schedule. Whatever system works best for you, keep it close enough to your phone so you can make notes as clients call you; set project deadlines; or schedule appointments. Always put everything directly and immediately into the calendar to help meet deadlines and stay on top of appointments, meetings, and tasks. The next section of this chapter goes into more detail on the different calendar management systems and the pros and cons of each.

4. **Go as paperless as possible:** An amazing thing about using your computer to manage as much of running the consulting business as possible is it can also reduce a major amount of paper clutter. Keep business files, invoices, and contracts on your computer. E-mail items instead of printing them out. You can even use a digital signature to sign documents and contracts before sending them to a client, so there is no need to print it out, sign it, fax it, and then have to worry about creating a file to house it. You can even turn hard-copy paperwork into digital files

by scanning and storing the document on the computer filing system. It is easy to accomplish a computer filing system with a program like Microsoft Word, where a file is created for each client and everything that pertains to the client can go in the file. Sub-files can also be created for organizing multiple projects for the same client. Once hard-copy papers are scanned and stored in the computer filing system, the hard copy can be shredded. This ensures that no stacks of paperwork are building on the desk, avoids making a mess, instantly files the document away in its place, is easy to access again when you need it, and is, above all, organized. Use an online backup system or back up files on a CD in case your computer fails.

5. **Do it now rather than save it for later:** Once the office is clean and organized, it is time to implement one final strategy of the organizational system: Anything that can be accomplished and put away now should be done immediately rather than setting it aside, creating clutter, and creating a mess. When you receive a piece of paper, do what you need to do with it and then put it in its place. When you pull out a project to work on, put it away before moving on to the next project. When you get into this habit, it becomes part of doing business and helps keep the organizational system up and running.

Manage your schedule

One of the primary benefits of managing time effectively is that managing your calendar and schedule pushes your business forward. Having a time-management system in place propels the consulting business forward. A lack of a scheduling system can be a hindrance and hold the consulting business back from success.

As mentioned in the previous section, there are several scheduling options available that range from basic to more advanced. Selecting the most appropriate option depends on your type of consulting business, technology budget, and personal preferences. Here is a closer look at a few options, along with the pros and cons for each system:

The calendar

The simplest method available for scheduling is the written paper calendar. Whether a wall, desk, or other type of calendar, it is easy to use, inexpensive, and does the job of keeping track of appointments, meetings, and important dates. Use a pencil so items can easily be erased, rearranged, or changed. The biggest downfall of a wall or desk calendar is that it is not portable, so it cannot easily be put in a briefcase or purse and pulled out to consult when communicating with clients when you are on the go. Another drawback is that paper calendars have space limitations, so it is difficult to write everything in the space available.

Day planners

A day planner is a step up from a calendar because day planners tend to be portable, depending on the style and size. Additionally, day planners provide advanced options for organization, using a tabbing system to separate months and to divide the calendar portion from the address book and other sections that typically come in a day planner. Some day planners even have compartments for housing small papers, business cards, and paper clips.

Some of the other benefits to using day planners come with some of the sections included in the day planner, including places for lists, notes, expense sheets, and car mileage records. Some day planners also have a section for keeping addresses and phone numbers, or even a calculator.

One of the major drawbacks of a day planner is that everything is written: appointments, tasks, contact information, and other records. Another problem is you have to carry your day planner, which can become heavy with all of the paper inside of it. It can also be risky to keep personal and professional information stored in a single place because if you lose it, you lose your entire system, from your calendar to all of your contact information.

Electronic systems

Another way to organize schedules, contacts, and notes is with an electronic system. The computer, a personal digital assistant (PDA), and cell phone are all electronic options for tracking the same information as a day planner. From using free calendar and contact systems online to synching your portable electronic device with your computer, the options are almost endless and extremely convenient.

One advantage to an electronic system is that you can easily back it up, so you always have backup files. Another advantage is that you can share your calendar and other information with virtual assistants, employees of the consulting firm, vendors, clients, and anyone else you choose to give access to this information. Finally, electronic systems typically come with everything you need to manage your office from one device, including a calendar, task list, notes section, contact management system, e-mail, and Internet.

The main drawback of using an electronic system can be the cost. If you do not already own a computer, software, or smart phone, then you may have to purchase one or more of these items to get started. Computerized scheduling can do anything you need it to; consider the cost and how it fits into your budget so you can invest in features and software products you need that are also affordable. On the other hand, it is easy to argue that electronic systems can save so much time that this supersedes the cost.

CASE STUDY: ORGANIZATIONAL TOOLS AT WORK

Breakthrough Enterprise LLC
Kerri Salls
Westford, MA 01886
978-692-5258
www.breakthrough-enterprise.com

Kerri Salls and Breakthrough Enterprise LLC serve startup and established solo businesses. The target market is anyone over 40 with experience and expertise who wants to grow and thrive in his or her own business in any economy. Solo businesses can be consultants, startups, sole practitioners, solopreneurs, entrepreneurs, and small businesses.

In order to overcome the challenges of running her own business, Salls uses three critical tools to stay on task. She also teaches these tools to her clients. First, she creates a "Six Most Important Things List," which sets her focus on the six most important things that she must get done each day. Second, she uses a weekly plan sheet, where she blocks out time in all areas of her life on a weekly basis to be sure everything gets done and she meets all of her work priorities. Finally, Salls uses a 12-month wall calendar for her projects and marketing plans for the whole year.

Business manager role

As a "solopreneur" consultant, you not only play the role of the worker bee, but you also have the responsibility of managing the business. Managing a business requires a changing of roles throughout the day. One minute you may need to be the secretary, and the next minute you are the bookkeeper paying the company bills and vendors. In between it all, the consulting work also has to be handled. Essentially, a business manager is responsible for every task that it takes to make sure the business is operating according to plan. The role includes a wide range of responsibilities that stretch from customer service to making sure that all of the bills are getting paid — even if this simply means that the accountant is receiving a copy of invoices and bills that need to be paid.

So, how can you manage both sides of the business effectively and without completely losing your mind? The answer is that it all comes back to learning how to manage your time wisely and effectively. Divide the day up into consulting work and business tasks. While the consulting work is what brings money into the business, dealing with the administrative task of sending out invoices also brings money into the business. When creating a daily schedule, schedule time in to handle both sides of the company: consulting and business management.

Delegating responsibilities

At some point, as your business grows, it will come to a point when managing all of the tasks on your own is counterproductive. For some consulting companies, this happens right from the beginning. Other consulting companies expand into the need to either hire additional employees or outsource work that can be delegated.

For most home-based consultants, building a virtual support team is the answer. This allows the owner to delegate roles, responsibilities, and tasks without having to have a full-time staff. Virtual staffing allows you to keep expenses down because there is no need to rent bigger office space, buy furniture, or create expenses such as phone lines and computer equipment. In addition to the cost savings, hiring virtually opens up the pool of talent worldwide because you are not limited to the applicants that are currently living within a driving radius of your business.

If a social media expert is needed to handle your social media marketing campaigns, you can find the best social media expert that you can afford and hire her — we will call her Susan. It does not matter she lives in the Greek Islands because she works when she wants from the comfort of her own home or office. Her expenses remain her expenses, and the consulting business's expenses remain the consulting business's expenses — minus the fee you have to pay the social media expert for her services, of course.

Experts argue that putting a virtual support team in place when establishing the business is the most beneficial strategy for any small business. It sets the tone for the business by allowing the consultant to focus solely on consulting and revenue-generating activities, while each of the virtual support team members focus on what they do best, which also indirectly generates revenue for the business. Virtual roles may include:

- Virtual assistant (VA)
- Social media marketing expert
- Marketing manager
- Public relations manager
- Web designer
- Graphic designer
- Accountant
- Sales manager
- Database manager
- Advertising

☐ Checklist

☐	Decide which time-management and organizational systems to put in place.
☐	Create a daily schedule prioritized by deadlines and project urgency.
☐	Devote a balanced amount of time to consulting work and managing the business.
☐	Determine if you want to start your business by building a virtual support team, or decide at which point in time your business needs to start delegating duties to employees or virtual team members.

Chapter 9

Building Your Brand

In this chapter, you will:

- Learn how to build a brand around you as the consultant, your skills, and your company's unique offering.

- Discover brand building techniques consultants can use both online and offline to build their brand, credibility, and business.

- Create a positioning statement.

- Craft your marketing messaging.

- Discover logo design opportunities and the need (or not) to have a business logo.

- Learn how to create other marketing collateral such as business cards, a website, brochures, and a marketing kit.

- Uncover how to build the marketing foundation for finding and attracting clients to the consulting business.

Building a brand around you as the consultant and the specific services your consulting business provides involves a myriad of factors, including the spirit, personality, slogan, values, look, feel, and benefits the consulting company, its representatives, its products, and its services portray. When building a brand, focus on connecting with the target audience; the brand you build should reflect how you want the target audience to feel when they see your business card, website, or logo. Building a brand is about appealing to all five senses

To find the brand essence of your company, the next few sections walk you through the process of uncovering the right look and feel for the consulting business. As you go through the steps, also keep in mind that branding flows through to you as the consultant and any representatives of your consulting business. In fact, if the consulting business is based on the experience and skills of the consultant, then brand building may revolve around the consultant himself or herself, because in reality, the consultant is the business.

Character

The first step in the brand process is to determine the character of the company. As a consulting business, how should the business feel and act? What does the business like, and what does it dislike?

A good example of company character is the Walt Disney Company. Disney has created an entire product line, theme parks, and more all based on being the happiest place on earth. Disney's character is fun, whimsical, and magical. This character shines bright in everything Disney does, sells, and supports. From its talking mouse, Cinderella Castle, and giant teacups to spin around in, fun and whimsical are the overriding themes of anything Disney.

Branding for a consultant business may be more on the serious side as compared to Disney, but maybe not. If a consulting business helps playhouses create set designs, then it is possible that imagination and fantasy trickle into the company brand.

The character of the consulting business is the foundation for the next step in the brand building process, which involves the relationship between the business and its customers: This is customer relations. When a customer purchases an alarm system from a security company, he or she feels safe. When someone walks into Disney, it makes him or her feel happy, fun, or young again. What feeling are you trying to convey to your clients? Jot down on a piece of paper any adjectives that describe the feelings that your business should conjure up in the minds of your customers.

Aesthetics

When it comes to branding, there is also a visual component; it must be aesthetically pleasing to prospective and current clients. The visual components of branding are items such as a logo, character or mascot, color schemes, and font styles. Visual branding can work one of two ways. First, you may build a relationship with a client, and when he or she sees the visual representations of the company, it may reinforce the feeling he or she has about working with your business. Second, a prospective client may see the visual components of the company and either be intrigued enough by what he or she sees to learn more, or get turned off by what he or she sees and move on.

In a way, visual branding is similar to meeting someone for the first time. A person may be judged by the way he or she looks, but once you get to know that person, what you see and what you feel may not match. In branding a company, however, it is important that you match the look of the business components with the way you want customers to feel about your company. For example, when you see a big, yellow, bouncing smiley face talking about rolling back prices, visions of Walmart and its low-cost quality goods probably come to mind.

Think about and write down how your company logo, colors, font styles, and other representations should reflect the values, morals, strengths, and benefits of the consulting business. These representations should trigger a response from prospective and current clients when they see them so that they recognize your business and services instantly.

A small side note here. Branding at the level of a Walmart, Target, Disney, or Coca-Cola may or may not be in reach for your consulting business. The key element here is not to create a huge conglomerate in the consulting world, but rather to create a connection between your consulting business and the people, businesses, or organizations that can benefit from the services it provides. After working through these three steps, you have to connect each element of the branding process in order to create a brand for you as the consultant, for the consulting business, and for the services it provides. The company brand is the bridge between the company and its customers. It is possible to create a bridge that keeps attracting repeat business.

Branding is Perception

Many companies create a brand based on how they want their customers to feel and connect with the company, products, and services. Unfortunately, it is not always about how a company wants its customers to feel. In reality, a brand is really about how current and potential customers perceive it to be. Finding the balance between how you want your brand to be perceived and how it is actually perceived is the key to successful branding.

For example, a nonprofit organization built a brand around helping battered women make it on their own by providing job training, business suits, and interview skills to help them land new jobs and start new lives. Potential donors of the organization, however, thought the organization existed to help an entirely different group of people. Because the perception was different from the reality, the nonprofit continuously struggled with raising enough money to fund its programs and initiatives.

When brand perception is off-balance for a for-profit business, it can be even more important because it may mean the difference between running a profitable consulting company and having to close the business forever.

Three Ways to Balance the Brand with Audience Perception

1. Create and write a mission statement for the company that is understood and memorable.

2. Survey potential and current clients to see what they think the company does — what products and services it offers. If this matches the purpose of the company, then the brand and brand perception are in balance. If not, adjustments need to be made so that the balance is restored.

3. Segment messaging with the audience. No matter what type of consulting business you have, chances are you have several different market segments you cater to. When creating a brand and messaging, make sure this aligns with the audience you are targeting. For example, a wooden hanger manufacturer has two different audiences: high-end customers and budget-conscious customers. For this reason, it has two different Web pages. One page speaks to and sells to the high-end clientele while the other speaks to and sells to the budget-conscious clientele. It is all about how the copy is written, the price of the hanger, and how the hanger is branded to match the needs of the customer.

Customer perception is everything when it comes to branding. You can hire the most expensive branding company in the world to design your logo and create a brand for your business, but if the company brand and customer perception do not match, then it is all just a waste of time and money.

Creating a mission statement

One aspect of company branding is the company mission statement. Writing a mission statement mystifies most business owners, but a mission statement is not as baffling as some may think. When it comes down to the basic purpose of a mission statement, understanding its purpose makes writing it a simple, fast, and easy process. A mission statement is typically one or two sentences explaining why the company exists, the purpose of the company, and what the values of the company are. If you are drawing a blank in writing a mission statement, these three easy steps will help you break down the writer's block and write a compelling mission statement that does your consulting company justice.

1. **Focus on purpose:** Many business owners tackling the task of writing a mission statement think the mission of the company has to be long, drawn out, and complicated. This is not true. You can and should be able to describe why your company exists and one of the key benefits customers have from working with the company.

2. **Focus on fulfillment:** Writing a mission statement and being able to fulfill it are two different things. Writing a mission statement is not about writing it for the sake of writing one. The company also needs the ability to fulfill the mission statement, so be realistic about the mission statement as well. For example, an environmental organization may have a mission statement that says, "to make the world a safer place to live." This statement alone does not have much meaning attached to it because it is not clear as to how the company is going about making the world a "safer place to live." The Florida organization Save the Manatees focuses its world saving efforts to one area of the world, the water, and one animal in the sea world, the manatees. Hence, the mission of Save the Manatee is, "Our mission is to protect endangered manatees and their aquatic habitat for future generations."

3. **Write it down:** The first two steps were thought-provoking processes to encourage you to think about the purpose of your business and how you can go about fulfilling that purpose. Now it is time to put your mission statement into words and down on paper. Remember to keep the mission short, simple, and to the point. Your goal is to be able to hand the mission statement to complete strangers and have all of them understand what your company does.

Brand your business for modern times

Before the widespread use of Internet marketing, branding applied to tangible marketing collateral such as brochures, business cards, and letterhead. Modern times, however, have opened up the door to entirely new branding issues that directly relate to other marketing collateral such as websites, blogs, and social media networks. Modern times call for modern measures, so here are some branding exercises to walk through when evaluating the company brand online and offline.

Be search engine friendly: Controlling the message current and potential customers see from your business is as important online as it is offline. Who does not sit down at their computer and use a search engine to find information out about companies, products, and services? When writing copy for the company website or posting blogs and articles online, make sure to include words in the copy that customers would use to find the services the consulting company provides. It is also important to control the name of the business by buying the domain name of the business and the top five variances. Variances may include buying the .com, .net, and .us versions of the domain name or other variances such as the business name spelled out completely, the business name acronym, and any other names your company goes by. If your consulting business does not include your name, for example, you may also wish to purchase your name as one of the domain names. When customers conduct an online search for your business name, this helps to direct them to the consulting business website — even if all five or six domains point to the same website. You want to control the information someone sees when searching for your business, which is also being in control of the company branding.

Write and post with care: Publishing online is pretty easy to do. In some cases, it is too easy, which can cause a company branding problem. When you write and publish something online, it stays there forever, even if you delete it. Be careful what you say when you post something online. Make sure it reflects what the consulting business stands for and sheds a positive rather than a negative light on your business. Make a good first impression, and avoid racy or potential problematic photos or statements.

Match tangibles with intangibles: Branding requires consistency. This means the same colors, logo, look, and feel run through all of your marketing collateral — website, e-mails, online banner ads, print ads, letterhead, brochures, and business cards.

Personal and company image

In a consulting business, the consultant's image and reputation can speak volumes to potential and current clients. If you miss appointments or deliver incomplete or work of poor quality, the client may leave with a bad impression of you and the consulting business. Not only does this affect the current project, but it also puts the possibility of obtaining any future projects in jeopardy. Most organizations refer businesses that have done a good job for them, so make the right impression the first time. It can help you land one project and many more to come.

Image is much more than the way you handle projects. Reputation and professionalism both play an important role in image as well. Ethical behavior and trustworthiness are characteristics clients are willing to pay a higher fee for to receive. Creating a good image and reputation is an ongoing process, but there are several things you can do to start off on the right foot.

A book is judged by its cover (and pages)

Creating a professional image is about what you look like on the outside and the professional way you come across to people when you meet them. While you may be a genius in your field, if you show up at a client meeting in wrinkled clothes, with your hair standing up, and coffee on your shirt, clients may be put off by your appearance. Being a professional starts from the outside and works its way in. Acting in a professional manner also adds to an image. Be aware of using foul language, bad habits, and other rude behaviors. Work on correcting these habits and personality traits — even if it means creating a work persona that you put on when you talk to clients on the phone or walk into their office for a meeting.

What to do to create a professional image

- Minimize any negative aspects that could be misconstrued as unprofessional, such as body language or appearance.

- Be honest with clients. Let them know what you can and cannot do, and be honest about project needs. This earns the client's respect.

- Dress professionally. Wear what you would expect the client to be wearing, or better. If you look sloppy, clients will believe your work is sloppy and will refrain from working with you.

- Under-promise and over-deliver. Do not make promises you cannot keep. Always clearly state what you can and cannot do. It is better to tell a client that something cannot be done and then end up pulling it off for them than telling them you can do something that you cannot deliver.

- Connect your personal image with the business image using marketing collateral such as business cards, letterheads, and report covers that represent you and the company.

Reputation

A reputation is even more important to potential and current clients than image because a bad reputation can damage an image. Several key areas affect the reputation of a consultant. The primary element of a reputation is the work quality. Second in importance is the way the consultant presents in public. Both of these elements help to build a positive and high-quality reputation rather than a negative and bad reputation. Remember, it is easier to maintain a good reputation than to have to overcome a bad reputation. Once you do something to hurt your reputation, it takes twice as much work to get back on track, and you may never fully recover. Therefore, it is imperative that you take steps necessary to maintain the best reputation possible.

One way to build a positive reputation quickly is to always perform your tasks and complete projects to the best of your ability. Because consulting in the industry or niche you are working in is your passion and area of expertise, this should not be hard to do. Make yourself readily available and easy to talk to, and keep the lines of communication open with your clients. Community involvement can also be a reputation booster. Volunteering and working in the community allows you to shape a positive reputation while also doing good deeds. For example, if you are starting a tax consulting business, offer your services pro bono to non-profit organizations for a cause you support. If you are a Web design professional, offer a free seminar to teach local businesses how to get their businesses on the Internet. Write and submit news pieces, editorials, or articles that offer a unique and interesting perspective to major newspapers and magazines within your field. For example, as a financial planner, offer a piece on debt management to a family magazine. Write a book on an aspect of your job and career. Getting your name out in the areas where your customers are is one of the best ways to build a high-quality reputation.

Weaving the Brand Together

Once you determine the look and feel you want to use to represent your personal and company brand, the most important aspect of branding is weaving it into every aspect of your consulting business. Branding encompasses everything that is internal and external with your company, so whether it is a memo that goes around to the internal employees of the consulting business or an e-mail that you are sending out to the client list, the brand standards apply. Some of the items you need to consider when applying the business brand include:

- Company logo
- Business cards
- E-mail signature
- Letterhead
- Brochures
- Marketing kit
- Website
- Blog
- Mailing envelopes
- Promotional items such as pens, magnets, and notepads
- Proposals
- Client agreements or contracts

Marketing messaging

In order to start building a solid marketing foundation, one of the first tasks you will need to tackle is to determine your marketing message. A marketing message is the signal you want to send to your current and potential customers about your services. Some marketing professionals refer to this as a positioning statement because it is a written statement that "positions" your company and how you want it to come across to clients.

So, a positioning statement for a celebrity life consulting firm may be something like, "Zesty Life Consultants is a lifestyle resource offering practical resources and coaching programs to celebrities seeking to transform their life from less than optimal to exquisite. Unlike other lifestyle consultants, Zesty Life Consultants provides a step-by-step system and access to Zesty Living Designers that coach their clients through the process to achieve their unique, ultimate lifestyle."

After you get your positioning statement in order, then you want to establish one to three key messages you want to send to current and potential customers through your marketing efforts. These key marketing messages directly promote the products or services that you are touting for your business, but they are not taglines or memorable and catchy phrases. Instead, these are the messages that you want the audience to walk away with after reading your marketing collateral.

For example, Zesty Life Consultants may have these three key messages:

1.   Zesty Life Consultants offers a proven system for creating exquisite lifestyles: The 7 Practices for Optimal Living.

2.   Zesty Life Consultants provides useful resources and easy-to-implement tools to guide celebrities on their journey to living a Zesty Life.

3.   Zesty Life Consultants offers coaching programs with Optimal Life Designers to help clients fast-forward their journey to living a Zesty Life.

To create your own key messages, list the three primary products or services you plan to offer your clients. Under each service, list out how the service benefits clients. Now form messages with the services and the service benefit that you want clients to walk away with after exposure to your marketing initiatives.

Logos

Using a business logo is part of the branding strategy of the consulting business. While a business logo is not as essential to a service-based business such as consulting as it is to a product business where product packaging is involved, many consultants opt to have a logo designed for their company.

You have several different avenues you can take to obtain a logo for your consulting business. First, you can hire a graphic designer to create a custom logo for your business. Generally, logo design of a custom logo starts at $200. There are also companies that sell ready-made logos, which you can purchase for as little as $25. These logos are not customized to your business and may be sold to many other companies to use, so it is a logo that is not exclusive to you. The benefits of buying a ready-made logo are that it is inexpensive and offers you an opportunity to create a brand for your business with the logo.

Finally, you can use software programs such as Microsoft Publisher or other desktop publishing programs to create your own logo. These programs typically have ready-made logos that you can use as is or personalize to fit your needs. If your design skills are up to par, you can also use these programs to create your own logo from scratch.

Business cards

Business cards are another marketing essential. You will need business cards for a variety of purposes that range from handing them out at a networking event to including one in a marketing kit you send to a prospective client.

As is the case with creating a logo, there are a variety of ways you can design and print business cards for your consulting business. The most expensive way to obtain business cards is to hire a graphic designer to design the business cards and then send the file off to a printer to have the cards printed. Websites such as Vistaprint (**www.vistaprint.com**) and 48hourprint.com (**www.48hourprint.com**) bring customized and professionally printed business cards down an expense level. These sites have professionally designed business card templates you can customize, personalize, and print at a reduced rate. You also have the option to upload your own design, so even if you have a graphic designer create the card, you can upload the card to print through one of these companies to professionally print the cards for less than most local printers will charge.

Desktop publishing programs also make business card templates available for you to create business cards. You can print these cards on your own printer using business card stock you can purchase at any major office supply or stationery store. While this may be the least expensive way to get the business cards you need, it does require a time investment. Another disadvantage to creating and printing your own business cards is that it may cheapen the image of your company.

Website

Having a business website is an essential component of conducting business nowadays. Getting your business website up and running boils down to two main options. You can either build and maintain the website yourself or hire a professional to build and maintain it for you.

A myriad of options exist online for website companies that offer templates you can use to customize the look and feel of your business site. Other sites allow you to host your website with them and build your own website with a desktop publishing or design program such as Microsoft Publisher or Adobe® Dreamweaver. Taking this route may cost you anywhere from $4.95 per month to about $50 per month, depending on the website host you choose and the service options you choose to utilize through the host — such as memory storage amount, e-mail addresses, template options, and domain name.

The other main option is to hire a website designer to custom design a site for your business. The cost for a custom website design can run you anywhere from $100 for more of a basic website to thousands of dollars for a complex website. Not only do you need to consider the cost of hiring a designer to create your consulting business website, but most designers also charge you for making changes to the site after it is up and running.

If it is within your budget, choose a custom site for your initial design, although this will make any changes and maintenance that needs to be done difficult. Let the professionals do what they do best: build a great website. After the design of the website is settled, you also have to consider how you are going to obtain the content for the site. You either have to write the content on your own or hire a writer to create the content for you. This can be an added expense of anywhere from $100 to thousands of dollars, depending on how many Web pages of content you need the writer to create for the site.

Brochures

Some consultants — the ones who meet more face to face with clients or the ones who send physical marketing packages to clients — find it helpful to have a company brochure. Brochures can be used in various marketing initiatives, from handing them out at tradeshows you may attend to including them in marketing kits to media professionals or potential customers. Consultants that focus more on online marketing typically replace a hardcopy brochure with an electronic format option. A third group of consultants uses a combination of an online and hard-copy brochure.

As is the case with creating a logo, there are a variety of ways you can design and print business cards for your consulting business. The most expensive way to obtain business cards is to hire a graphic designer to design the business cards and then send the file off to a printer to have the cards printed.

Vistaprint and 48hourprint.com also provide customizable brochure templates and printing options. These sites allow you to design your own brochure, add the content, and print the quantity you need at a less expensive rate than most local printers. You can also opt to have the brochure designed by a professional or use desktop publishing software to create your own brochure layout and then upload the design to one of these websites to print the brochures.

Finally, you can buy brochure layouts that are scored for folding at your local office supply or stationery store. Use a desktop publishing program or templates to customize your brochures, and print them using your home computer and printer. While this method can be highly cost-effective and you can print brochures as you need them rather than having to order hundreds or thousands at a time, it is important to make sure that the brochures do not lose the professional appearance you want them to have. If your brochure looks anything less than professional, it may turn clients away from working with you, which is the opposite of the effect a brochure should have.

Marketing kits

For service-based and high-ticket items such as consulting, you have to impress potential customers a bit more than a tangible product-based business in order to get them to buy. Putting together a marketing kit provides your consulting business with the opportunity to impress, motivate, and sell by providing your audience with more information than is possible to fit on a business card or in a brochure — or what you could say in an elevator pitch.

Marketing kits can be a powerful tool to convert sales; leave the kit as a takeaway from a client meeting, or drop it in the mail as a follow-up to a phone conversation or in response to an e-mail request from a prospect for more information. Always include two business cards and a company brochure, if you have one. A marketing kit is a comprehensive tool providing information to prospective customers that goes beyond handing them a business card and brochure alone. There are a few key essentials needed for your marketing kit:

Folder: In order to build a marketing kit, you need a folder or some sort of holder for the marketing kit information. Keep in mind that the container the marketing kit comes in is the first impression your customer receives, so you want it to look professional. You can accomplish this in one of two ways. First, you have the option of having folders professionally printed for less with online printers. A less expensive option is to have a label professionally printed that you can then affix to a linen pocket folder that can be purchased at any major office supply store.

Marketing template: In order to weave the consulting company brand through all of the marketing pieces, you will next want to create a marketing template. A marketing template is the layout that each piece is printed on that is then included in the marketing kit.

USP: Earlier in this book, you learned about creating a unique selling proposition to make your consulting business stand out from competitors. Make sure that your USP is included as part of the marketing kit information. Make sure you word it so that it shows how your company can benefit your customers from the customer's point of view.

Sell the benefits: Most consulting businesses and businesses in general provide a list of features rather than the benefits a client enjoys by working with their company. When you list a consulting service in your marketing kit, make sure that you are listing out how this service benefits the client by revealing how it resolves an issue.

Service offering: Include a bulleted list that allows the customer to see your service offering at a quick glance. Follow the bulleted list with a more descriptive list of the consulting services your company offers.

Testimonials: Customer testimonials can sell your services better than anything you can say to prospective customers. Include a full page of customer testimonials, or have your customers record testimonials that you then include on a DVD or CD as part of the marketing kit.

Articles or media coverage: Third-party endorsements from the media can also pack a powerful sales punch and should be included in the marketing kit. Include reprints of articles published about your company; DVDs of media interviews; or newspaper, magazine, or online article clips where you have been quoted as an expert source.

Now that you have the foundational tools ready for marketing the consulting business, the next chapter covers how to attract clients to the consulting business.

☐ Checklist

☐	Create the company and your personal brand.
☐	Craft a unique selling proposition (USP).
☐	Use brand-building techniques online and offline.
☐	Create a positioning statement.
☐	Craft a company and marketing messaging.
☐	Decide if a company logo is needed. If so, have one designed.
☐	Make a decision on how to create and print marketing items such as business cards, a website, brochures, and a marketing kit.

Chapter 10

Finding Clients

In this chapter, you will:

- Create the marketing plan portion of the business plan.

- Learn ways to attract your target market with online marketing tactics.

- Discover offline methods for attracting the audience you are after.

The marketing plan is really the action part of your business; these are steps you can proactively take in order to market the business, make people aware that the business exists, and find new clients. There are two sides to every marketing plan, which covers online and offline tactics you can use as a consultant to attract the clients that fall into your target market and have those clients hire you. Ultimately, you can use the marketing plan as is to get started. The thing with marketing plans is that they are dynamic documents because after you implement the plan, you have to go back and evaluate the success or failure of your marketing tactics. Once you analyze the results, you can then tweak and adjust the marketing plan that needs to be implemented for the next six months to a year.

One important factor to keep in mind is that marketing a consulting business is a process. You cannot conduct a marketing activity one time and then decide that it is a complete failure because you do not see immediate results. You must take consistent action in implementing your marketing strategies for at least six months to a year.

The first part of the marketing plan is the marketing strategy. For a consulting business, three marketing strategies exist. Commit these three strategies to memory because every marketing activity covered in the remainder of the plan hinges on these three strategies.

1. Gather qualified leads and followers in order to grow your subscriber list and database.

2. Nurture the qualified leads and followers in your database by consistently getting in front of them, in various ways, with information about your consulting services.

3. Convert the leads into clients and generate revenue by introducing them to your consulting services.

Marketing Foundation

Before you can start to implement and integrate the various marketing activities set forth in the marketing plan, you first have to build your marketing foundation. *Building your marketing foundation includes putting together the marketing pieces and collateral, which was discussed in detail in Chapter 9.* Because the first half of the marketing plan covers the online activities you can partake in to attract client, the consulting business website needs to be up and fully functioning so that you have a venue to drive traffic to when marketing your consulting services online.

In order to build the brand of the consulting business, which tackles the first marketing strategy, there are a few implementation strategies to include as part of the website in order to grab the attention of your ideal client. Traffic should be driven to the website from a variety of venues, which will be discussed later in the plan. Driving traffic to the home page of the website will be an important first step to gathering leads and converting them into clients. It will set the stage for learning more about these prospects and then up-selling them into the next logical service level you offer that fits their needs.

By incorporating certain elements into your website design, you can increase the credibility of your consulting website, allowing you to gather highly targeted leads that can be further qualified and turned into more revenue for the business. The following are elements your website should include:

Entice with an irresistible free offer: Offer an incentive to help capture information on the visitors to your website. An irresistible free offer can range from a free downloadable report on a topic of interest to them. In exchange for the visitors to your site providing their name and e-mail address to you, provide something to them for free. Capturing these leads is the key to building your database of prospective clients. If visitors to your site are interested in accepting your free gift in exchange for providing you with their information, then they are potential customers for your business — at least upfront. The rest of your marketing activities help you to further qualify these leads and eventually move them into client status.

Further qualify subscribers: As part of the subscription process, add a one-question survey to the free offer subscription. Use a question that directly relates to the challenges your clients may face. For example, a private school consultant that helps parents and clients maneuver the private school application, acceptance, and financial aid process may ask, "What is your biggest question about the private school admissions process?" The point of the question is to find out what your prospects are thinking, feeling, or seeking information about. You can then use the information you gather to create solutions that cater directly to what clients and prospects are seeking.

Ensure comprehensive branding: Make sure that your branding is carried throughout all of your Web pages, auto-responders, and other marketing collateral for consistency purposes. Use the same color schemes, font styles, layouts, and templates throughout all of your materials.

Optimize your pages: Use keywords in the copy of your website that prospective clients would use to search for the products or services your consulting business offers; this is the basis of search engine optimization (SEO). Choose one or two keywords to focus on for each page of your site, and then scatter the keywords, phrase, and combinations of the phrase in the beginning, in the middle, and toward the end of your copy. Make sure that the copy is written to include the keywords so that text flows and sounds natural. You can use free keyword tools such as the Google AdWords™ Keyword Tool, or you can hire a professional keyword consultant to help you come up with a list of keywords to include on the site.

If you provide services to a confined geographic area, be sure to include keywords that speak about the area you cover. You should also use the keywords in the page titles, headlines, and sub-headlines in the copy on each page.

Internet Marketing and List-building

A growing business requires you to steadily grow your existing database by gathering highly targeted new leads. This creates the foundation for significant business growth and increased revenue for your consulting business. Once you fill your database with the ideal prospects you seek, you can then work on selling them your paid products and services by communicating with them on a regular basis. Here are some ways to keep your clients up to date:

E-newsletter: Regularly publish an e-mail newsletter to create an automatic lead-capturing system online and as a communication tool for your existing database.

Editorial calendar: Create an editorial calendar to map out discussion topics for the next six weeks or so. Block out time on your calendar each week to create this content and post it on your blog. You can also use existing content you have — such as products, presentations, and reports — to break down and turn into blog posts. Each blog post should be approximately 200 to 400 words. The editorial calendar can also be used for creating e-newsletter articles and social media updates.

Social media

Harnessing the power of social media outlets drives more targeted traffic to your website, which in turn will drive more clients for your consulting business. This provides you with the opportunity to communicate with your target market on a more regular basis and in different ways, and it can have a powerful and positive effect on growing your list and your consulting business. Social media networks include Facebook, Twitter, LinkedIn, and YouTube. Each social media network works slightly differently, so you will need to familiarize yourself with each one. The following sections, however, go into detail on how you can utilize each network as part of your social media marketing efforts. You can implement the following social media strategies:

Facebook Fan Page

Create a Facebook Fan Page that speaks directly to your target markets and focuses on the geographic area of your business (if applicable). On the fan page for your business, you can also include an opt-in box for your free offer so that visitors can immediately subscribe to your list and be taken to your website. To build your fan base, include a special announcement in your e-newsletter to drive traffic to the fan page. Be sure to include a link to your fan page in every piece of correspondence you have with your prospects and client. This way, you are creating a two-way street: driving traffic from social media to your website, and vice versa. If you can gather video or audio testimonials from clients, these are also great ways to let your services speak for themselves. If not, then record case studies or scenarios where you can illustrate how your service helped a client to gain success.

You can use the Facebook Fan Page in various ways, including sharing your blog posts with links to drive visitors directly to where the post sits on your site and posing questions to your audience in an effort to engage them and make it more of an interactive experience. This also allows you to evaluate who your audience is on your fan page so you can then work on funneling them into the appropriate service level of your business. You can also integrate your Twitter™ account with your fan page so that your updates get more exposure. You can even have a custom background created that matches your brand in addition to the sidebar information about your business. A dramatic or attractive background can boost interest for followers.

Facebook profile

Because Facebook limits actual profiles to individuals, it is better practice to create a Facebook Fan Page or group for your consulting business and integrate your personal Facebook page with your business's page. Use your personal profile page to talk about your professional relation to the business, join relevant groups, and RSVP to events that connect to your target market. Join groups or become a fan of any professional organizations you belong to and any of your competitors. Also, integrate your Twitter account with your profile so that your updates get more exposure.

Twitter

Twitter is another social media marketing tool you can use to promote your consulting business online. Use Twitter to share information, products, and services related to your business. This helps to position you as an expert resource for information without always trying to sell them on your products and services. Aim for 80 percent information sharing and 20 percent promotion. You can integrate your tweets with your blog posts and articles, which is a highly effective way to attract followers, and it permits you to communicate with your followers and drive them to your website. Almost all tweets should include a link to a specific blog article, product, or service on your website. Sharing helpful tips or information on Twitter has to be done within the 140 characters that Twitter allows for messages, also known as tweets. Make your tweets intriguing, and then send your followers somewhere they can get more information by including a link. Twitter allows you to share information, but your goal is to use it as a tool to drive traffic to your consulting website — as is the goal with all of your social media marketing. Be sure to use the "shorten URL" feature on Twitter to keep the length of the URLs as short as possible; bit.ly (**http://bit.ly**) is a URL shortener that also tracks your links, giving you information on how active a certain post is.

Follow people you admire — such as authors, bloggers, e-zines you read, seminars you attend, or leaders in your field — as well as your competitors. Visit these profiles and their lists of followers to find people to follow who fit your target market. Consider having a custom background created that matches your brand in addition to the sidebar information about your business. A dramatic or attractive background can boost interest for followers.

LinkedIn®

LinkedIn is another online source for professionals, business owners, and entrepreneurs that can develop your consulting services. Add a direct link to your website's home page in your profile so people can take advantage of your free offer right away. Your LinkedIn profile should connect to your blog for further exposure of your content. You can start connecting with individuals who are in related businesses. This is a great way to connect with possible joint venture partners, potential clients, and other referral sources. Also look for people located in the geographic area your business covers, if applicable. This is a great way to connect with potential clients as well as referral sources.

LinkedIn provides a built-in application for gathering recommendations from clients you have worked with or other professionals on LinkedIn who you have done business with. Spend some time once per quarter gathering recommendations from your contacts. LinkedIn can be a very powerful tool, especially after you have connected with at least 500 other professionals. Even if you cannot get recommendations, you need to use LinkedIn as a tool to connect with your target audiences. Integrate your Twitter account with your profile so that your updates get more exposure.

YouTube®

Create and use a free YouTube account to upload instructional videos that speak on a certain point of interest to your target audiences. You can also turn each of your written blog posts and/or e-newsletter articles into a video. You are providing just enough information to encourage your audience to gain more information by going to your website. These videos can also be added to your Facebook profile and fan page for additional exposure.

Remember, you want to be everywhere that your target audience is, and these are the social media sites your target market is using.

Blog

Having an up-to-date blog is the No. 1 way people are going to find your consulting business online because search engines look for updated content when determining page rank. Share your expertise about your business, industry, or niche in your blog posts. Then, integrate your blog with the social media sites (Facebook, LinkedIn, Twitter) to help drive traffic to your site. Mix it up between longer, more word-driven posts talking about industry specific news and shorter posts about a new product or service. Any videos or images you can add will also help make your blog more three-dimensional. Just remember: Your blog should not be just about your business; you want to connect with your clients, not hard sell them your services. You can use complimentary blogging platforms such as Wordpress (**www.wordpress.com**) or Blogger (**www.blogger.com**) to create and maintain a blog.

In order for a blog to be an effective marketing tool, it is imperative for you to post on your blog at least two to three times a week. Blog posts should include keywords your potential clients and target markets use to find information on the services you provide.

You can also map out a year's worth of e-newsletter content, tweets, and public relations campaigns that are all built around the same editorial content topics to keep everything streamlined and in alignment.

Article marketing

Use content you have created and develop it into new articles — aim for at least one article per week. Popular topics for consultants include how-to articles and articles that cover specific steps or detailed information on topics relevant to your audience. For example, a business consultant may write an article on the top five ways to make sure that your business succeeds its first year in existence. A marketing consultant may write an article on the top seven ways to drive targeted traffic to a business website.

You can use these articles to disseminate information via your e-newsletter, upload them to article directories, such as EzineArticles (**http://ezinearticles.com**) and Amazines (**www.amazines. com**), use them on your blog, and post them on your social media networks. Make sure your articles are also rich with keywords. Article marketing is one of the most effective and least expensive ways to drive targeted traffic to your consulting website. Your goal in using article marketing is to drive visitors to the appropriate page of your site — where your free offer sits. Your goal is to get them to request the free offer in exchange for gathering their information. You do this by including a strong call to action in the resource box of each article you submit online. This is also a lead-in for other marketing communication efforts and up-selling to your paid services.

You can also record the articles you write and repurpose them into videos and podcasts. Upload the podcasts to your blog and create an audio or video series that you can include on your blog, distribute in your e-newsletter, upload to YouTube, or send out as a special series of e-mail blasts to your subscriber list. Podcasts can also be uploaded and distributed on iTunes.

Link building

On a weekly basis, visit the business websites, blogs, and forums that are related to your business, niche, or industry. These are additional places where your audience is looking for information and another place where you can find information, as well as start building relationships with other consulting companies. Post a relevant, valuable comment on at least five sites per week. Forums and blog posts allow you to post your name, business name, and a link back to your website — again, driving traffic back to your site. This is an indirect way of promoting your business by positioning yourself as an expert and a resource while creating additional exposure for your business. You want your name, company name, and website address all over the sites that have anything to do with your business. If your potential clients are visiting these sites, you want them to see you there too.

Sites of this nature may also offer an opportunity for you to become a guest author or article contributor, which allows you to use content you have to share your expertise with a new audience, gain the attention of your target market by positioning yourself as the expert you are, and broaden your reach.

Direct response

You also need to focus on nurturing the existing leads you have and the new ones you are gathering by consistently communicating with your database. You can communicate with your database by sending out your auto-responders and promotional e-mails at least once or twice a month. Promotional e-mails may include a special offer on one of your consulting services, announce the dates of an upcoming teleseminar, or incorporate a case study that illustrates a problem one of your clients faced and how your services resolved the problem. Promotions and case studies can also be included in the e-newsletter you are sending out to the database.

Traditional Marketing is not Dead

Now that you have a variety of ways you can market your consulting business online, it is time to take a look at the avenues available for marketing your business offline.

List building

While there are numerous ways you can build your list using online marketing tactics, there are just as many ways you can build your list with offline marketing tactics. In fact, the best way to build your list is to combine your online and offline list building efforts. Some of the ways you can build your list offline include:

- Be a guest or participate in as many teleseminars as possible.

- Be a regular guest on various Internet radio shows.

- Advertise with organizations and associations that are targeting your ideal clients.

- Interview well-known people in your niche and post these interviews online and in print publications.

- Submit articles to print publications your target market reads.

- Advertise in print publications your target market reads.

- Add your free irresistible offer to the back of your business card.

- Do a postcard mailing to a high-quality mailing list.

- Attend live networking events and seminars that cater to your target market.

- Periodically ask past and current clients for referrals.

Public relations program

One of the key programs that will help to boost your business and subscriber list while increasing credibility is publicity. Publicity is a low-cost, effective way to reach your target audience. The purpose of publicity for a consulting business is:

- To inform potential clients and referral sources about you, your company, your services, and how you can help them.

- To educate the media and potential clients in order to shape attitudes and behaviors and change perceptions about your industry.

- To effectively communicate your marketing messages.

Public relations (PR) is one of the easiest, most cost-effective ways to promote who you are and what you do so you can get more clients and more sales for your business. PR builds credibility and visibility that helps you gain new customers and clients and can increase your income. Public relations is the art of building favorable and profitable interest in you, your business, or your service by creating a "buzz" in the marketplace. PR gets your message across and tells others about you, what you do, and why it is important to them. Public relations lends credibility to you and builds your reputation from a third-party point of view; therefore, it is often more valuable than advertising alone. PR is effective because it:

- Creates awareness of your brand.
- Communicates the benefits of your products and services.
- Positions you as an expert.
- Generates sales and leads.

PR is usually free and lends more credibility to your claims. It is the most cost-effective way to generate interest about your consulting business and reach existing and potential clients. When people read about you in the media from a journalist or hear about you on the radio, you get instant third-party validation and receive positioning as an expert in your field. While a paid advertisement placed in a publication can cost you tens of thousands of dollars each time it is run, a well-placed article is much more cost effective and adds value to your business.

Trade publications have a number of subscribers, and most have thousands of readers, each of whom is a prospect that may need the services your consulting business offers. At the very least, the readers likely know someone who needs the services you provide. In addition, this positions you as an expert, which produces a premium price for your services because people are more willing to pay more for your expertise. This often removes price as an obstacle to overcome in the process of attracting new clients. PR also levels the playing field and allows small businesses to appear larger than they are and compete on the same level as larger businesses.

PR helps you attract qualified prospects and leads. The more people know about you, the higher the level of trust it builds, which makes it more likely they will contact you and refer others to you. As an added bonus, current clients get the confirmation they need that your business is the best one to do business with. Here is how to get started:

Develop a media list: A media list should include local and national outlets that will have an interest in covering your story. It is important to find individual reporters, journalists, and writers for the publication that would have an interest in covering your story. You will need to gather and maintain a PR contact list for these local journalists and publications, either by paying for these subscriptions or doing independent research online.

Implement editorial calendars: Most print publications publish a calendar outlining topics they will be covering throughout the year, called an editorial calendar. Use the editorial calendars of your top media outlets to help you to develop story ideas for promoting your business. These lists are useful when pitching story ideas, so you can tie in your story with these topics. Also monitor and identify publicity opportunities from journalists and lists such as Help a Reporter Out (**http://helpareporter.com**), Pitch Rate (**http://pitchrate.com**), and Reporter's Source (**www.reporterssource.com**). By responding to a reporter's source query, you are establishing yourself as an expert in your consulting niche. Your credibility and reputation can only build if you are positively quoted in a news article.

Write a pitch: Your pitch should be personalized to the person you are pitching the story to. Mention similar stories they have covered, or point out why their readers would be interested in the story you have to tell. The pitch should also include an overview of the story and have the press release attached for more details.

To start, determine the top three local media outlets for newspaper, TV, and radio in the area where you run your consulting business. Send press releases to specific journalists or editors, and follow up accordingly.

Write a monthly press release: You should send out one press release per month for special events, workshops, or webinars you are promoting. An easy strategy if you do not have something specific to promote for the month is to use your blog or monthly e-newsletter articles as a press release. This way, you leverage your writing and are able to use your content in multiple places and for multiple purposes.

When writing a press release for online media, the main goal is to get keywords picked up by search engines. A search engine optimized press release is geared toward specific keywords rather than a specific story idea. SEO press releases are written and used online in order to increase the amount of traffic you drive to your website. Keyword-focused press releases are generally distributed through wire services. Many companies — especially larger ones — are sending press releases through these online services for the primary purpose of driving traffic to their websites. Submit your monthly press releases to the top five online press release distribution sites, which includes one paid service and four free services.

ONLINE PRESS RELEASE DISTRIBUTION CHANNELS	
www.PRWeb.com	$80/release
www.I-newswire.com	Free
www.IdeaMarketers.com	Free
http://Free-press-release.com	Free
http://24-7pressrelease.com	Free

Pitch to the media and follow up frequently: Once a month when you write the press release, pitch the story to the appropriate media outlets. Follow up with each media contact you have pitched the story to, and make sure they received the information. Use the follow-up as an opportunity to see if they are interested in covering the story.

Speaking opportunities

Speaking opportunities can be an excellent source for new prospects and sale conversions for a consultant. You can use speaking opportunities to expand your reach and position yourself as an expert in your field. Off-site speaking engagements help you reach potential clients while simultaneously enforcing the establishment of your expertise. Some options include being a guest speaker for radio shows, webinars, and workshop.

Speaking engagements allow consultants to connect face to face with current and potential clients and referral sources. It provides the opportunity to showcase areas of expertise, schedule appointments with potential clients, and even close sales.

Have a system in place to gather the names and contact information of the attendees of the show or event where you are speaking. Run a contest to gather attendee names, e-mail addresses, and telephone numbers; this allows you to build your list of leads and provides you with the opportunity to follow up with those leads to try to convert them into clients.

Speaking engagements are also prime locations for selling services on the spot. Run a show or speaking engagement special so if a prospect becomes a client at the show, they receive a special discount or bonus offer.

Write a book

The purpose of writing a book is to promote your expertise. You can write and self-publish a book using a print-on-demand website (such as **www.lulu.com** or **www.cafepress.com**) on a topic that is hot in your industry. You can sell the book on consulting websites and at public speaking engagements. Book sales are another lead-gathering tactic, where you can then communicate with book buyers to convert them into a consulting client.

CASE STUDY: THE EFFEC-
TIVENESS OF NETWORKING

Human Edge Resources, LLC
Eleanor M. Lyons
Newtown, PA 18940
267-566-0370
www.humanedgeresources.com

Eleanor Lyons worked in financial services for 16 years. She had negotiated a two-day per week telecommuting schedule with her company when her son was born in 1998. When he was about 8, her company experienced a reorganization and she was informed that her telecommuting days could no longer be accommodated. She had always wanted to start her own consulting business, so Lyons and a colleague left their jobs to start Human Edge Resources, LLC in March 2007.

Lyons uses Microsoft Outlook to schedule her appointments with clients. She even schedules her time to design and develop plans for clients to make sure she is balancing all of the aspects of her business. When business is slow, she reaches out to ten contacts per day through e-mail, phone calls, and meetings. She has found that networking is extremely important when you run a consulting business; it has been the most successful tactic for attracting and landing her ideal clients.

Networking has been so successful for bringing in new business to Human Edge Resources because it leads to business referrals. When Lyons and her partner first started the business, they created a spreadsheet that contained all of their contacts in the business world, and included personal contacts who worked at organizations that fell into their market strategy. Every two months, they send out a newsletter, which includes insights and tips on particular topics.

Using their network has worked best to grow their business because they are out meeting people on a regular basis through organizations such as the local chamber of commerce and some women's business groups. Most of the work they do comes from referrals — all from word-of-mouth advertising and the newsletters they e-mail to their database. They have not spent any funds on more formal advertising.

☐ Checklist

☐	Implement the marketing plan portion of the consulting business plan.
☐	Attract your target market by consistently implementing online marketing tactics.
☐	Attract members of your target audience by simultaneously implementing offline methods in conjunction with your online marketing tactics.

Chapter 11

Client Interaction

In this chapter, you will:

- Learn about the various touch points you will have with clients.

- Discover effective ways to interact with the client starting from the point they contract your consulting services and throughout the entire project.

- Uncover post-project communications to help elicit repeat and referral business from the client.

- Find out some of the specific ways to tell clients that what they have been doing is not positively impacting their business and encourage them to implement necessary changes.

While all of your marketing efforts are touch points with your prospects, once you sign an agreement with the prospect, from that point on you are interacting with a client. Landing a new client is one vital side of your consulting business, but working with the client in a professional manner in order to keep the client is the other integral part of running a successful consulting business.

A solid foundation of success for any consultant is having a high-quality level of communication with the client from the very beginning. Communication includes both the verbal and written communication you will have with a client as a consultant. If you start off with open lines and effective forms of communication with the client, it will make working with the client and working on the client's projects a much easier, smoother process. Effective communication is the key to any solid business relationship, so it is imperative that you learn how to communicate and interact with clients at the various touch points that take place before, during, and after the project begins.

Luckily, effective communication is something that you can learn. Practice makes perfect with acquiring and refining your communication skills, so if you are not a strong communicator, make a concerted effort to get your communication skills up to par.

Written Communication (Before the Project)

Written communication is just as important as verbal communication, and putting items in writing can even help to clarify and solidify the information, so as to avoid problems and misunderstandings later.

After the proposal is out of the way and the client wants to pursue working with you, your next step is to provide a written contract or agreement to the client that spells out the details of your working relationship. As you will quickly see, a contract is essential for any consultant working in virtually any field because putting the agreement in writing details precisely what your role is in the transaction, what the client's role is, the payment structure, and other terms and conditions that must be met.

A contract includes every important detail, including what the project entails, all the specifications of the project, the time line, and the payment details. Another important aspect of the contract is a termination clause, which provides a way for either party in the transaction a way to end or terminate the agreement. For example, if the client is not happy with the quality of the work, a termination clause spells out the specific steps the client has to take to end the agreement. The same holds true for the consultant.

As you work with the client, if situations change or the scope of the project you have been hired for changes, then the contract or client agreement also needs to be changed. You and the client need to have a conversation about what the changes are, and an addendum to the contract needs to be created and agreed to by both parties. For example, if additional work is added to the project specifications, outline the changes in the addendum to the contract. Always put changes in writing, and have your client agree to the changes before proceeding.

Contracts are legally binding, which is why it is important that everything is in writing and that there is a signature from you and the client on the contract. *You can reference a sample contract on the CD-ROM to see what a contract can and should contain.* You can use the sample agreement as it is, or you can modify it to fit your needs. After the contract is in place, begin to work with the client on the project at hand. Once you start working with the client, both verbal and written communication are involved in taking the project from the contract stage to completion.

Six Essential Methods of Communication

Aspects of communication are numerous, and all forms of communication cannot be exhausted in this book. However, there are six areas of communication specific to consultants that are necessary for you to take heed. Communication is similar to a well-oiled machine, so while each part of communication is separate, in totality, the communication efforts must work together in order for the overall relationship to function properly. Utilizing these six methods of communication will help you to solidify successfully completing each client project.

Tip 1: Carefully choose your words

Most of the time, it is not what you have to say to a client that is the important part, but rather *how* you say it to the client. Think about what you are going to say before you speak. Once you know what you need to say, make sure that you word it in a way that does not sound negative, combative, or give off the wrong impression to the client. For example, rather than say, "You are doing it wrong," say something less abrasive, such as, "Have you ever approached it like this...?"

Do you see the difference? You are saying the same thing, essentially, without attacking the client — or at least making the client feel like you are attacking him or her.

Tip 2: Ask questions first

Gathering information from the client at the beginning of the project sets the stage for the rest of the project. If you jump right in offering the client suggestions without first asking all of the right questions, then you may end up embarrassed. Never make assumptions about clients or what they have tried before hiring you as a consultant. Instead, ask questions of the client in order to garner the information you need. Gather all of the facts and lay them out in front of you before you assume what the client expects out of the project.

When you ask questions, really listen to the client's responses. Clients provide you with many clues with what they say, so rather than formulating what you are going to say in your head while the client is talking, make sure that you fully understand what the client is saying. Repeat back to them what you interpret to make sure that you understand correctly.

Most clients are more than willing to answer your questions, but some are more resistant than others. If clients resist fully answering your questions, simply explain that there are several different ways to accomplish the project, and your questions are simply for clarification purposes to make sure that you implement the most effective strategy.

Tip 3: Be enthusiastic

To each client that hires you, his or her project is the most important one of all your projects. This means that even if this is the 100th time you have worked on a similar project, you have to be enthusiastic about tackling this client's project. While there are times that you will simply sit and listen to what the client is saying, your body language, responses, and facial expressions have to portray excitement rather than disinterest and boredom. Keep eye contact with the client, smile, and show your interest in what the client is saying every time you meet with him or her.

Tip 4: Keep it simple

Consultants tend to use jargon and lingo that pertains to their specialty but means nothing to the client they are speaking to. When you talk to your clients, you need to address them in a style and manner that makes sense to them. You will also run into clients who like to receive different information in different ways, so you are going to have to read the client so that you are responding to their needs. For example, some clients want to know all of the details no matter how small. Other clients only want you to tell them what they absolutely need to know and nothing more. Try to disseminate information in small chunks so that it is easier for the client to take in and to process.

Tip 5: Be a good listener

A popular saying is that humans have two ears and one mouth for a reason — to listen. When you are working as a client consultant, it is paramount that you listen to precisely what your client is saying. You can only accomplish the project and fill your client's needs if you know what those needs are. Be an active participant in a conversation in the client, so say what you need to say and share with him or her, but also actively listen to what he or she is saying to you as well.

Tip 6: Get to know your client

Find the right balance between getting to know your client professionally and getting to know the client on a personal level. Getting to know your client better can help make you communicate better with him or her. For example, if in a discussion you find out that the client is more of a morning person, you may want to schedule your meetings and phone calls with the client during his or her peak performance times. If you learn that the client has children who play sports, you may want to occasionally ask how they are playing. It is important not to go overboard, but mixing some personal and professional time can deepen your relationship with clients.

The Right Way to Ask Questions

Rather than sounding like a drill sergeant, blurting out questions to a client machine-gun style, there is a fine art to asking questions in a way that does not make you seem overbearing. You have to be able to ask clients questions in order to uncover the details of each project. Questions can also help to clarify information you already have to ensure that you understand the project. Nothing wastes more time than launching into a project to find out later that you did it wrong because you did not understand all of the facts. It is not just a waste of your time when this happens, but it may also lose you the client. Here are some tips and approaches you can take when it is time to weave some questions into your client interaction.

1. Set a goal with your question

It may seem like a leap at first, but one of the first questions you should ask a client is what his or her expectations are at the end of the project. What results are he or she trying to achieve? This is a goal-setting question, so once you know what your goal is, it is much easier to fill in the steps required to get your client from where they are today to where they need to be as the project comes to an end. In reality, you should know the answer to this question before you start working with a client. Typically, this is a question that happens at the courting stage of the relationship, but it is also a good idea to clarify that the goal is the same when you start to work on the project. Your belief of what the goal is and the client's belief of what the goal is must be the same or the results may be way off course. If your proposal does not meet their needs, chances are good that they will overlook you.

2. Lead into a question

Preface your questions by first sharing information with the client. Position yourself as the expert you are by sharing knowledge and experience about the question you are about to ask. Then pose the question at the end. For example, you may use the lead-in, "Did you know that…" Sharing some information with the client upfront sets the stage for the question you need the client to answer.

3. Repeat for comprehension

Once a client answers the question, reform the follow-up question so that it repeats the client's responses in order to make sure that you comprehend what the client is saying. For example, if the client tells you three different goals he or she wants to accomplish with the project you are undertaking, then you may ask, "Can I go over the goals with you again to make sure that I understand?" Then go through the goals one at a time and how you interpreted what the client said to make sure you are both on the same page.

4. Get the client to make a decision

Throughout the process of working with a client on a project, you are going to come to points where the client needs to make a decision. Even once the client tells you which choice they make, you may want to make sure that this is the path they are committed to. You can phrase the question to be something like, "Are you committed to..." or simply restate the answer for clarification purposes. It is not about repeating exactly what the client says back to them like you are a parrot. It is more about allowing the client to hear what they are saying to make sure that what they are saying and what they mean are the same thing.

5. Mix up open- and close-ended questions

Find the right balance of closed- and open-ended questions to ask the client. Yes and no questions only get so much information out of a client. Too many open-ended questions, however, can make the client feel like they are doing all of the talking. Both types of questions call help you gather the information you need, so use both versions of questions to attain the information you need. Use both open and closed questions. Yes and no answers only work for confirmation, whereas open-ended questions encourage them to share details, providing you with the information you need to make key decisions.

6. Leverage answers for new questions

Use the answers a client provides to a question to formulate another question. This methodology works best for clarification questions, especially if the client gives you an answer you were not prepared to receive. Using the response to ask the next question helps you to uncover the true meaning behind the response and to make sure you understand what the client is saying.

7. Approach from a different angle

If you ask a question, but the client does not provide you with an appropriate response, then you may have to ask the question again from a different angle. Rather than saying you do not understand the client's response, simply compose the question in a different way to try to get the answer you need.

8. Get down to the nitty-gritty

Clients may glaze over a question you ask or give you such a broad response that it is not enough information for you to go on. Be straightforward with the client and really dig deep to get to the details. For example, if the client gives you a broad response as a goal, then ask a question to start narrowing down the focus of the goal. You may even want to ask the client, "What do you see as our first step?"

9. Be prepared

Each meeting or discussion you have with a client should have a specific purpose. You should always conduct your own research and go to the meeting prepared to accomplish the goal set for the meeting. For example, if you are helping the client to develop a website that is similar to that of one of their competitors, then you should spend time on the competitor's site. You will have an idea of what the client wants and a list of questions ready to talk with the client to make sure you take the website development in the right direction.

Listening is Just as Important as Talking

What you say is as important as the information you take in from the client. As much as you can work toward refining your communication skills, there are also steps you can take to improve your listening skills.

Be an active listener: To be active, you need to participate in the conversation, so while talking may not be necessary, you need to react to what the client is telling you. Keep eye contact, shake your head, smile, or show an expression of surprise. Whatever is an appropriate reaction, make sure that you are fully engaged in the conversation when you are the listener.

Stay focused: It happens. People start blabbing on and on about a topic, and your thoughts start to wonder. When you are listening to what a client is saying, you have to stay focused on the client rather than think about what you are going to have for lunch or the host of other tasks you could be tackling right now rather than listen to this client. When your thoughts are not on the conversation at hand, you are not focused, so clear your mind of everything except what the client is saying.

Take notes: Jot down notes or ask the client's permission to record your discussions. It is impossible to remember everything a client says, even if you are intently listening. Taking notes makes you a better listener because it forces you process what you are hearing to jot it down on paper. Taking notes creates reference material that you can refer to later and throughout the project.

Ask more questions: Responding to what a client says by asking a question illustrates that you are listening and even makes you a better listener because you are waiting for the response to your question. Asking questions and listening go hand in hand. The process is a give-and-take situation between you and the client. By listening and asking questions yourself, you can be sure both of you are on the same page.

Effective Report Writing

Written reports are updates you provide to the client to let the client know where the project stands. While you may have a discussion before or after (or both) you send a written report to a client, it is important that reports are detailed enough to provide information such as what stage the project is currently in, as well as any setbacks, changes, or progress made on the project. Reports should provide a high level of detail to make sure that the client has all of the information necessary and to prevent misunderstandings that can occur.

Clients may request weekly or monthly updates or as certain milestones of the project are met. You may want to spell out report submission terms in your contract. Other times, consultants simply provide reports to client on a regular basis or upon request from the client.

Nine times out of ten, your consultant reports and updates will be sent via e-mail. In fact, even if you provide a client with a verbal report, you should send the written report as a follow-up to your conversation. For example, your client calls you on your cell phone to get an update of what is happening with the project to make sure the project is on target. You can provide the client with an update on each point of the project, but when you return to the office, send the client an e-mail that starts off with something to the effect of, "Per our conversation earlier today…" and then outline the details of the update you provided. Written reports make communication clear and precise, so it is worth investing the time it takes to write the report.

The key element a written report must possess is organization. A clearly organized report encourages the client to read it, while a disorganized and complex report can discourage a client from reading it. Write a concise, detailed, and effective report to help ensure the client reads it and receives the essential information the report contains.

When it comes to writing these reports, there are various aspects to take into consideration. In fact, as a consultant, you will use these reports as a way of communicating as well as relaying your needs. Therefore, you need to write reports correctly to communicate with your client.

Writing progress reports

Think back to your school days. When teachers sent home progress reports each quarter or semester, the report provided your parents with an update on where you stood with grades, assignments, and behavior. The report either gave you a green light to keep doing things the same or a warning that it was time to make some changes before report cards came out. Progress reports do something similar for clients in that they give the client a status report on the project and provide the client with the ability to ask you to make changes, as needed, to achieve the goals of the project.

The length and style of consultant progress reports are not set in stone, so the report can be tailored to fit the needs of your business or the needs of the client. If a one-page report provides all of the details, then use a one-page report.

Always be upfront and honest in your reports. If there is a problem, you want to bring it to the client's attention sooner rather than later. You can put the client relationship in jeopardy if you try to hide things or gloss over things in your report. You can and should include pertinent information in the report. Here are some ideas on specific areas that are typically covered in a consulting progress report as it relates to the progress status of the project.

Overall summary: Start out with an overall summary of the status of the project. You can spell out the accomplishments on the project to date and let the client know the current status of the project.

Outline of accomplishments: Because the summary is a brief overview of the accomplishments of the project, the next section of the report is a more detailed outline of the project accomplishments. Provide as much detail as possible without being redundant. Provide the client with information on what you have been working on since the last progress report.

Completion status: Next, provide a client with a list of the completed tasks. Include the task description, date of completion, and what percentage of the overall project is complete.

Outline tasks to be completed: Then, outline the tasks that are pending, in order, so that the client sees a picture of what is left to be done.

Issues or concerns: If you encountered problems, let the client know what the problems were and how you did or did not overcome them. This provides the client with an opportunity to examine the problem and help you find a resolution. This is a great area to list the challenges you have faced and how you have overcome them and also to ask for assistance.

Set expectations with your clients on progress reports at the beginning of your relationship. You may also want to spell out the report schedule in the contract or in writing for the client. Reports may be something clients want and expect, or it could be something they are not interested in receiving. Plus, if you outline the time frame between progress reports — for example, once a week — the client knows when to expect the next report.

Writing final reports

While progress reports keep clients abreast of the situation along the way, the final report is the one provided to the client when the project ends. While a final report signals the end to one project, it may be the starting point of another project.

The final report is similar to a progress report, only without looking ahead. It should also include a few other details and informed opinions you may have regarding the project. These reports can be an outstanding way to convey your message to the client about future projects they may need. Sell yourself here, letting them know what you believe is the next step. A final report includes:

Summary: A summary is the best place to start and provides the same information the summary does in a progress report. Outline the overall accomplishments you made during the project and the ones that were not resolved. The summary is a brief overview of what you will go into detail about later in the report.

Outline: Outline the overall scope of the project and what the original goals of the project were. You can also include the methods you used to accomplish the goals and what your role in completing the project was.

Approach: Give a detailed explanation of how you approached the project, showing the client that you have done everything you could to successfully move the project forward.

Recommendations: The end of one project is often the beginning of a new project, so if there are future opportunities the client should know about, make your recommendations and suggestions in this section. For example, if you designed a website for the client, the recommendations may include suggestions for expanding the website, for growing the readership, or steps to take the website to the next level.

Conclusion: The final portion of the report should illustrate what you accomplished and why it was important. Show how the completion of the project has benefited the client.

Post-project Communication

When a client project ends, this does not signal the conclusion of your relationship with the client. Clients can be sources of repeat business and referral business, so even when projects end, your communication opportunities with past clients should continue.

Maintaining an up-to-date database of contact information is vital so you can continue to send information to clients. One of the first items you should provide to a client along with their final report — or after the final report — is a survey.

Surveys allow you to gather information and feedback from the client on your service. Good feedback can be used as client testimonials to help you land new business. Poor feedback or constructive criticism can help you to make necessary adjustments to continue to make your consulting business better and better.

Current and past clients are one of the best sources of referrals. Because a customer has firsthand experience working with you, when the experience is positive, they can became a raving fan for you. You can make it easy for current and past clients to refer new clients to you by implementing a formal referral program. Referrals can be one of the best routes to take when developing a financially sound business because they are already qualified leads for you.

A formal referral program can offer incentives to clients who send you referrals that turn into clients. Spread the word about your referral program with satisfied clients as projects draw to an end. You can also send out reminder e-mails or announcements to old clients to rekindle relationships.

☐ Checklist

☐	Understand how to interact with clients at different parts during the project.
☐	Survey customers to gather feedback on your service.
☐	Implement a referral program.

Chapter 12

Building & Growing
Your Business

In this chapter, you will:

- Learn how to build credibility and create passive income.

- Learn how to create a team of experts to help you in your business.

- Learn how to handle moving or upgrading your office location, or establishing an office that was once home-based.

- Discover how to juggle multiple client projects at one time.

As you continue to work as a consultant, you will start to gain momentum. You will gather more and more clients, and you will probably work for some of your clients on more than one project. Some of your clients will send new clients your way through referral. All of these activities help to build your business. Some consultants choose to keep their business small and continue to run it out of their home on their own. Other consultants take on enough business to require additional consultants, along with administrative and marketing help. Some consulting businesses even transform into multi-million dollar corporations. You can grow your business from a small consulting firm to a bigger one by expanding your client base. In some cases, you create additional business without taking on any more consulting clients by becoming an information mogul.

Informational Products

Consultants are essentially information moguls because their service involves sharing their expertise and information with their clients to solve problems. This means there are several ways consultants can build credibility and generate passive income simultaneously. Some of the options for creating passive income include:

Live workshops and seminars: If you cater to a local audience or want to invite people from different areas to one location, you can sell tickets to live workshops and seminars. You can use these live events to share valuable information with your audience. Live events are also great places to sell your other products and services and to gather qualified leads to up-sell at a later date. Be sure to implement a system where you can collect names and contact information from attendees. Run a contest or offer a drawing prize as a way to gather this information.

Webinars: Webinars are online versions of live workshops and seminars. Webinars allow you to broaden your audience to anyone in the world that has a computer with Internet access. Some consultants use a free webinar as a lead-in to attract an audience and then up-sell the attendees on another product or service with a strong call to action at the end of the webinar.

Teleseminars: Teleseminars are similar to webinars, but as the name suggests, they are conducted over the phone. Attendees call a number and use a pass code that you provide to them, and then they use this information to get on the line at the scheduled time.

Keynote speaking at conferences and other speaking engagements: Conferences, associations, and other groups are always on the hunt for good speakers. If you can get in front of a room of your target audience at one of these events, this is a great way for you to build credibility. These are also prime locations for selling your other products and services.

Write and sell a book: Experts write books, so picking a hot topic in your industry that you can shine the light on or share your expert advice on can become a book. While you may be able to shop the book for publishing, you also have the option to self-publish the book in order to get it to market faster and easier.

Sell informational products such as CDs, audio files, e-books, and workbooks: You can record your teleseminars, webinars, and speaking engagements and sell these items online or at your engagements. That is the best part about something like a teleseminar or e-book — you can prepare it one time and sell it many times over.

Because these informational products are created once and can be sold over and over again, this is a great way to accomplish both goals — building credibility with your audience, and generating passive income.

CASE STUDY: MAKE YOUR SPECIAL INSIGHT WORK FOR YOU

Peter Zawistowski, consultant
North Reading, MA 01864
508-783-2488

Peter Zawistowski started his consulting business after being diagnosed with bipolar disorder and facing the challenges that trying to work as an employee presented when diagnosed with a chronic illness. He possesses special insight to this chronic illness, so he has transitioned into a business to help others like him.

Zawistowski works with individuals with bipolar disorder, with individuals who work with someone with bipolar disorder, and loved ones of bipolar sufferers. His work mostly concentrates on individuals who are self-employed or employed, helping them to deal with the situations and stressors that arise when trying to balance this disorder with life and work.

For Zawistowski, his own health reasons meant that self-employment was his only possibility for part-time or full-time work. By reducing the travel and related expenses that his previous employment and business created, his stress level has also been reduced greatly.

His clients are very information-focused, so he has found great success in creating passive income for his business and even attract new clients by offering information through webinars; writing and selling e-books; and writing, selling, and positioning white papers on various topics related to bipolar disorder.

Creating a Team

The ability to delegate is one of the prime characteristics of a leader. While many consultants start off as a one-person show in order to keep costs down until they can get the business to turn a profit, other consultants see the benefit of turning a profit faster by delegating duties to others sooner rather than later.

At some point in running your business, you will come to a crossroads where you are overwhelmed with work and need help. The degree of help you require can vary from consultant to consultant; it may simply be that you need help with administrative tasks, or you may need help in additional areas such as marketing, accounting, and graphic design.

You have two options for obtaining the assistance you need. You can either hire employees on a full-time or part-time basis, or you can outsource your needs to freelancers or businesses that can fill the role. If the consulting aspect of your business is more than you can handle, there may even come a time when you need to hire an additional consultant or two. Which route you take may be strictly for financial reasons. If you hire full-time or part-time employees, there are salaries and benefits that may become expensive for you to cover. You may also have to provide a place for them to work with a desk, computer, and phone line. Outsourcing and hiring freelancers, on the other hand, allows you to get the help you need without these added expenses. Typically, you are only responsible for paying them for the work that they complete for you.

Finding employees or individuals to outsource the work to can be a complex project because first you have to find qualified candidates, conduct interviews, and finally narrow down your options until you hire someone. Career and job websites such as Monster (**www.monster.com**), CareerBuilder (**www.careerbuilder.com**), and Monster+HotJobs (**http://hotjobs.yahoo.com**) allow you to post open positions in your company for a fee. You can also use free classified websites such as Craigslist, Kijiji, and BackPage (**www.backpage.com**).

Spend some time spreading the word with customers and colleagues about the type of people you are looking to add to your team. Some of the best employees can be found through people you know and people who know you and your business.

How to Move Your Office

If and when it comes to a point where your consulting business outgrows your home office, you will have to find office space to rent. Typically, upgrading your office occurs because you hire on employees that need to come into the office to work; therefore, you need space to house them. Consultants who start to work more on a face-to-face basis where clients come to their office typically need a professional office that is not in their home to conduct these meetings. Other consultants have personal situations with their home office that propel them to separate their work life from their home life, so they need to find an office and start the process of setting the office up.

Revisit Chapter 3 of this book for in-depth details on finding and setting up an office space that works for your business. Moving an office can be a stressful event, but there are ways you can reduce the pressure moving can put on your business. First, make sure that you think of every detail involved in the move. For example, pick a move date and time that is as unobtrusive to your business as possible. If you normally work during the week, then use a weekend to make the move.

Prepare the new office ahead of time by having phone lines and computer networks installed before the old office phone lines and Internet access are switched off. This allows you time to trouble-shoot without missing calls or e-mails. It is also imperative that you prepare your clients for the move before it happens. When you meet with clients in the time leading up to the move, let them know that you are getting ready to move your office in case they have trouble getting in touch with you. Send out an e-mail reminder to clients and the rest of your subscriber list to make them aware of the situation. You and any other company employees should also put an automatic response on your e-mails saying that you are in the process of moving the business. Voice mail greetings should also share this information with callers.

One of the biggest shocks that home-based consultants feel when they upgrade into an office location is the financial stretch. Going from paying zero rent to paying what may equate to thousands of dollars in rent each month is something you have to mentally prepare yourself to handle. On top of the operating expenses of the business, you will most likely need at least one employee to run the office when you are not there. This need adds the cost of paying a wage or salary, and maybe even benefits to cover the employee.

Conclusion

Now you have it: You have all of the tools and know-how needed to become a successful consultant. No matter what has influenced your move — a desire to be a business owner, being laid off from your job, being forced into early retirement, or seeking a more lucrative career move for you and your family — you now know how to resolve and overcome the challenges and obstacles of becoming a consultant.

Consulting work offers a rewarding experience where you sit in the driver's seat of your career and financial future. Making your own schedule, making your own decisions, and helping clients will empower you. Showcase your expertise by pulling answers from your own knowledge and experience, and then use this information to apply a solution to a client's problem.

It is not that you lack the knowledge to be a consultant. It is about combining your area of expertise with your ability to run a successful business. If you use this book as your guide, you are half-way there; now it is up to you to take the necessary steps to make your dream a reality. Keep this book with you as a reference as you work on putting your business together or when facing a challenge in your business; you will be able to use it for years to come.

Appendix

Sample Business Plan

Clayton Safety Solutions
BUSINESS PLAN — July 2010
Confidential

Development Team:
David Clayton

111 West Spring Street
Pimmit Hills, VA 22043
Phone: 555-555-9999
Fax: 555-555-1234
E-mail: dclayton@claytonconsulting.com

Executive Summary

This business plan describes the strategy for operating a safety training consulting business, named Clayton Safety Solutions, with an office located at 111 West Spring Street, Pimmit Hills, Va., 22043. The objective of this proposal is to outline the business's long-term marketing strategies.

Clayton Safety Solutions develops safety training, reporting, and compliance plans to help construction companies meet federal, local, and industrial regulations. David Clayton is available to travel to construction sites or business offices to evaluate client needs and oversee implementation.

Clayton Safety Solutions also provides on-site MSHA and OSHA safety certification classes, including first aid, hazard communication, confined spaces, mine safety, crane hand signals, heavy equipment, work ethics, accident investigation, fire safety, fire prevention, and hazardous materials.

Clayton Safety Solutions can help construction companies write or revise safety plans, evaluate current plans to identify areas that are not compliant with regulations or do not meet client needs, design safety and incident report forms, and set up safety report communication and storage procedures.

Unlike its competitors, Clayton Safety Solutions offers personalized turnkey services delivered by a highly experienced consultant.

By targeting operating construction companies with missing or functionally missing safety plans, Clayton Safety Solutions can increase revenue without substantially increasing expenditures. Clayton Safety Solutions will target this market segment through the "now is the time" advertising campaign in local trade publications and by encouraging word of mouth advertising and repeat business.

Objectives

Clayton Safety Solutions strives to make safety regulation compliance easy and affordable for small to mid-sized construction companies. By offering high-quality training and helping companies develop and implement easy-to-use procedures, Clayton Safety Solutions hopes to help reduce time and money lost due to preventable accidents.

Mission

It is the mission of Clayton Safety Solutions to help companies develop safety policies and procedures that go beyond compliance and actually improve employee safety. David Clayton is dedicated to staying up-to-date about construction safety and using their expertise to provide accurate, personalized, and effective safety information.

Keys to Success

Clayton Safety Solutions' success is the result of the following key characteristics:

- Thorough understanding of construction operations and safety concerns
- Up-to-date knowledge of best practices in construction safety procedures and policies
- Full-service safety training at the client's site
- Individualized approach to each client's needs
- Turnkey service in safety plan analysis, design, and implementation
- Extensive experience in construction and safety industries

- Nonjudgmental attitude toward construction companies with missing or functionally missing safety plans.

Statement of Purpose

This business plan has been designed to serve as an internal outline of the business's marketing plan and a guide to future development of the business.

Company Summary

Clayton Safety Solutions is safety training consulting business with an office located at 111 West Spring Street, Pimmit Hills, Va., 22043.

As construction companies face increasing requirements for safety training and accident reporting, owners, superintendents, foremen, and project managers can find ever-changing compliance standards hard to understand and costly to implement. Too often, safety standards are ignored until there is an accident or a client demands proof of compliancy.

Clayton Safety Solutions develops safety training, reporting, and compliance programs to help construction companies meet all applicable regulations. In order to make implementing a safety program as fast and easy as possible, David Clayton will travel to construction offices and sites within the Washington, DC, metropolitan area to determine client needs, evaluate current policies, and implement effective safety protocols.

In addition to helping companies develop and execute safety programs, Clayton Safety Solutions also provides MSHA and OSHA safety certification classes in the following areas:

- First aid
- Hazard communication

- Confined spaces
- Mine safety
- Crane hand signals
- Heavy equipment
- New hires
- Yearly refresher training
- Work ethics
- Accident investigation
- Fire safety
- Fire prevention
- Hazardous materials

Often, construction companies already have written safety policies. In this case, Clayton Safety Solutions can review existing safety plans and determine what new policies may be needed to comply with client needs or government regulations. Clayton Safety Solutions can also identify inconsistencies between written policies and field procedures and help construction companies implement best practices to minimize accidents and safety-related losses.

Company Ownership

David Clayton, owner of Clayton Safety Solutions, has been involved in construction management and safety training for 20 years. Clayton opened Clayton Safety Solutions in 2003 as a sole proprietorship. In 2005, Clayton Safety Solutions reorganized as a limited liability corporation.

Clayton earned a bachelor of science degree in civil engineering from West Virginia University and a master's degree in construction management from Bowling Green University. As a safety manager at a national construction company, Clayton received multiple trainer certifications from OSHA and MSHA. After being promoted to project manager, Clayton learned firsthand the challenges of applying safety policies in the field. After 15 years with his employer, Clayton decided to use his experience and expertise to help small and midsize construction companies design and implement safety plans that were realistic and effective.

Clayton is currently an active member of the Washington Metro Area Construction Safety Association.

Company Location and Facility

Clayton Safety Solutions operates from an office located at 111 West Spring Street, Pimmit Hills, Va., 22043

Legal Form of Business

The legal name of the business is Clayton Safety Solutions and operates as a limited liability corporation, as registered in the state of Virginia.

Services

Clayton Safety Solutions' services can be divided into three segments: safety plan review, safety plan implementation, and on-site safety training.

Safety Plan Review

Clayton Safety Solutions offers a comprehensive safety plan review package. As part of the review, David Clayton will analyze all aspects of a company's safety program, including:

- Existing policies
- Client requirements
- Federal, local, and industrial regulations
- Reporting forms
- Lines of communication

- Training certificates
- Inspection reports
- Construction practices

After the review, the company will be given a detailed reported listing areas where the existing safety plan can be improved or is not compliant with regulations or client requirements.

Safety Plan Development/Implementation

After analyzing a company's current practices, Clayton Safety Solutions can help develop and implement a comprehensive safety plan that can be put into place swiftly and followed without interrupting business practices. The safety plan development and implementation service includes:

- Designing customized inspection and accident reporting forms

- Establishing a storage method for reporting forms

- Listing certifications needed for each job description and writing a timeline for earning these certifications

- Writing policies that meet company needs and comply with current requirements

- Instituting a periodic review schedule to ensure the safety plan continues to be appropriate

- Safety training to update certifications

On-site Safety Training

Ongoing training should be at the core of any safety plan. Clayton Safety Solutions offers customized training classes at office or construction sites throughout the Washington, DC, metropolitan area.

Because David Clayton is passionate about providing the best possible safety training, his classes go far beyond the ineffective, "sit for a few hours and have your card signed" classes that other safety contractors offer.

A safety training session from Clayton Safety Solutions includes:

- Multimedia presentations designed to hold students' attention while teaching valuable safety practices

- Demonstrations and opportunities to practice safety techniques in realistic simulations

- A question-and-answer period where students can ask for clarification

- Case studies of real situations students may experience on the job site

Market Analysis Summary

According to the EMCOR Group, Inc., construction is the second largest employment sector in the United States.

Construction continues to be an important industry in the Washington metropolitan area. According to the Metropolitan Washington Council of Governments, more than 473 construction projects began in the area during 2007. Valued at nearly $6 billion, this marks the seventh largest year of construction since 1980.

After several recent high profile accidents, construction safety has becoming increasingly visible. According to the Bureau of Labor Statistics, 59.3 percent of OSHA investigation activities are focused on the construction industry.

Because of the rapid expansion of safety regulations, there is currently a high demand for safety consultants in the Washington, DC, area.

Market Segmentation

Since its inception in 2003, Clayton Safety Solutions has worked with three distinct types of construction companies:

- New companies with no current safety policies
- Established companies with existing safety policies
- Established companies with no current safety policies

Market Analysis

The following pie chart shows the percentage of income derived from each type of company by Clayton Safety Solutions over the past five years.

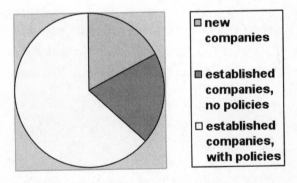

The majority of Clayton Safety Solutions clients are established companies with existing policies. Of these, 65 percent of the transactions are for safety plan reviews, 22 percent needed safety plan design and implementation (including safety training, if needed), and 13 percent required safety training only.

More than a quarter of the established companies with existing policies were returning Clayton Safety Solution customers. The pie chart below summarizes reasons given for repeat services.

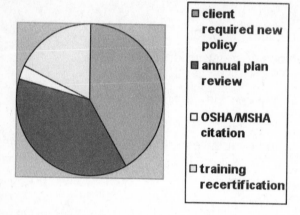

- □ client required new policy
- ▨ annual plan review
- ☐ OSHA/MSHA citation
- ☐ training recertification

Target Market Segment Strategy

Clayton Safety Solutions believes that established companies with no existing safety plan are an underserved segment of the construction company market. A telephone survey conducted by Clayton Safety Solutions of former clients within this market segment revealed the following:

- 72 percent discussed approaching a safety consultant for a year or more

- 76 percent lied about the status of their safety plan to potential clients or inspectors

- 56 percent allowed workers with outdated certifications to work

- 90 percent paid for certification training that they felt was inadequate in order to get a card signed

- 60 percent know of another construction company operating without a safety plan

- 98 percent delayed talking with a safety consultant because they were embarrassed about their lack of safety plan

- 60 percent were afraid a safety consultant would report them for their lack of safety plan

These statistics do not include existing businesses with safety plans so outdated as to be functionally absent. Taken together, businesses that are aware their safety plans are missing or incompliant are a significant portion of area construction companies.

By targeting this market segment and offering a nonjudgmental, under-standing, and friendly turnkey safety service, Clayton Safety Solutions can increase its revenue without a significant increase in overhead.

Service Business Analysis

New companies are more likely to need a turnkey safety plan service. More than 89 percent of new companies that contract with Clayton Safety Solutions require a safety plan review, design, and implementa-tion.

A surprising 20 percent of the customer base is made up of established construction companies with no safety policy. In talking with the man-agement, reasons for not having a policy include:

- No time to research requirements and write policies
- A safety program does not seem important
- The company just never had one
- Regulations are too confusing
- Clients have never required one

Of the established companies with no existing safety plan, 89 percent approached Clayton Safety Solutions because a potential client re-quired a safety plan as part of a bid package, 7 percent contacted Clay-ton Safety Solutions as the result of an OSHA or MSHA inspection, and 4 percent used Clayton Safety Solutions for other reasons.

Competition

Of the other safety consulting businesses in the Washington, DC, metropolitan area, only three actively market to existing businesses through industry publications. These offer cookie-cutter plans that do not take into account the company's specific needs or current practices.

One consultant offers complete plans in a day. While this quick turnaround will give construction companies a piece of paperwork to have on file in case of an OSHA or MSHA inspection, it does not allow time for a sufficient inspection of the company's needs nor for a full implementation of the plan. Instead, by using these consultants, companies are only receiving a generic safety plan with the construction company's name inserted.

None of the local safety consulting businesses that actively market to existing businesses offer turnkey safety plan development from analysis to implementation.

As the construction sector in the metropolitan DC area continues to grow, more safety consultants are appearing to try to handle the increased demand. Many new consultants have little or no experience in the construction industry. A survey of the websites of local safety service companies revealed that of the websites that listed consultants' education, 42 percent of consultants had only a bachelor's degree in a related field and 16 percent had a master's degree. The survey also showed that 77 percent had less than five years of experience in construction or safety management.

Strategy and Implementation Summary

Clayton Safety Solutions is poised to be a leading safety service provider to existing construction companies with missing or functionally missing safety plans.

Clayton Safety Solutions offers clients personalized plans, an experienced service provider, and turnkey services. This competitive edge combined with a targeted advertising campaign, word-of-mouth marketing, and increased repeat business will help Clayton Safety Solutions increase revenue within this market segment.

Competitive Edge

Clayton Safety Solutions will offer customized safety plans devised after a thorough analysis of each client's needs and business practices. Customers will be given plans that fit into their operations, are compliant with current regulations, and meet their clients' requirements.

With more than 15 years of experience in the construction industry, five years of experience as a safety consultant, and a master's degree in construction management, David Clayton has significantly more experience than the average safety service provider in the Washington, DC, metropolitan area. This experience allows him to understand the challenges of implementing policies on a hectic construction site.

Clayton Safety Solutions will continue to offer a turnkey safety service, guiding companies through the analysis, design, and implementation phases of the project with as little disruption to normal business operations as possible.

Marketing Strategy

Clayton Safety Solutions will institute a three-part strategy for increasing its revenue from existing construction companies with missing or outdated safety plans.

First, Clayton Safety Solutions will begin an advertising campaign with local construction trade publications. This advertising campaign will focus on the theme "You know you need a safety plan... Now is the time."

The campaign will stress the reasons for getting a safety plan and the benefits of using Clayton Safety Solutions, including David Clayton's experience, the nonjudgmental attitude clients will receive, and the high-quality, personalized turnkey service.

Clayton Safety Solutions will also institute a word-of-mouth campaign to encourage contact from new clients. Current clients will be given a 15 percent discount on future services when they refer another company.

In order to encourage repeat business from existing clients, ongoing safety plan reviews and recertification classes will be scheduled at the time of the initial service. Because clients will not have to call to arrange these important routine procedures, they will be more likely to follow through with safety plan maintenance services.

Bibliography

Biech, Elaine. *The Consultant's Quick Start Guide: An Action Plan for Your First Year in Business.* New Jersey: Pfeiffer 2001.

Nelson, Bob and Peter Economy. *Consulting for Dummies.* Indianapolis: Wiley Publishing, Inc., 2008.

Silberman, Melvin L. *The Consultant's Toolkit: High-impact Questionnaires, Activities and How-to Guides for Diagnosing and Solving Client Problems.* New York: McGraw-Hill, 2000.

Weiss, Alan. *Getting Started in Consulting.* New Jersey: John Wiley & Sons, Inc., 2009.

Weiss, Alan. *Million Dollar Consulting Toolkit: Step-by-Step Guidance, Checklists, Templates, and Samples from "The Million Dollar Consultant."* New Jersey: John Wiley & Sons, Inc., 2005.

Weiss, Alan. *Million Dollar Consulting: The Professionals Guide to Growing a Practice.* New York: McGraw-Hill, 2009.

Biography

A copywriter and marketing consultant, Kristie Lorette is passionate about helping entrepreneurs and businesses create copy and marketing pieces that sizzle, motivate, and sell. It is through her more than 14 years of experience working in various roles of marketing, financial services, real estate, and event planning where Lorette developed her widespread expertise in advanced business and marketing strategies and communications. Lorette earned a B.S. in marketing and B.S. in multinational business from Florida State University, and her M.B.A. from Nova Southeastern University.

Index